C000116966

AGENDA

Scentings

AGENDA

CONTENTS

CELTIC SAINTS

4

NOTES FOR BROADSHEET POETS

BIOGRAPHIES

Front cover: The Magic Apple Tree by Samuel Palmer.
© The Fitzwilliam Museum, Cambridge

Introduction

Welcome to this Scentings double issue of *Agenda* and many thanks to all contributors, readers and subscribers.

Apologies for the slightly longer than intended wait, but, on a personal note, the death of my treasured little horse – whom I had for twenty eight years – brought on pneumonia which is very debilitating, so the print date had to be put back.

I hope this issue of *Agenda*, like every issue, refutes what Jeremy Paxman recently claimed: that poets write mainly for other poets and are elitist. Some indeed do write abstrusely, if eruditely, for each other, but the poems chosen for *Agenda* are not in this category. Brendan Kennelly, for example, (reviewed here), has the facility to create poems accessible to uneducated, non-literary readers, yet which also speak to those well-versed in poetry at the deepest metaphorical levels.

I am sure you will agree that the poems here are written to communicate, albeit on different levels according to the interpretations that individual readers contribute to the poems. They are written urgently, to celebrate, to mourn, to commiserate, to refresh old perspectives, to render their own particular music. Rowan Williams, reviewed in W S Milne's essay, endorses this necessary kind of poetry. He defines poetry as imagination working at the highest pitch of language and attention. To him, poetry 'realises the given in a new way... pushing the inner tensions of language to the point of new discoveries in form and metaphor'. Many poems attempt to say the unsayable, to articulate the secret or reluctant parts of the human psyche not normally able to be covered in ordinary speech. As Rowan Williams adds 'poetic apprehension is essential to being a human self'.

Here, for example, is an immortal sonnet by **Josephine Balmer** inspired by the death of my horse, yet universalised:

The Horses' Grief

(after Iliad, 17. 426 – 446) for Patsy and Polka

Away from the battle, the horses wept,
realising they had lost their master,
their charioteer fallen in the dust.
In vain now Automedon tried to spur
them on with gentle words as well as harsh.
But they would not turn back. Like a pillar

standing tall and still on marble tombstone,
they were immovable, untouchable,
as they bowed their heads to the earth and shed
hot tears of grief for the rider they'd lost.
Their soft manes were matted as they shifted
their heads this way and back. Even the gods
were moved at loyalty only on loan
to men. Such ageless love. Immortal trust.

This issue, which happens to be a lot about rememberings, is also full of recent rememberings and honourings of special people in the poetry world who have passed on: Sebastian Barker, Dennis O'Driscoll, and, just as we are going to press, Felix Dennis. We wish them all a creative peace to rest in and for their words, wisdoms and spirit to sing on for ever.

The following elegy for Felix by Dr. **Christopher Fletcher**, Keeper of Special Collections in the Bodleian Libraries, Oxford, was sent in in the wake of Felix's death just two days ago:

Swallows

'They know me.'
Heat from hedgerow,
Thunderclap, then rain.

As another year thickens
I think of you
And your swallows

Dropping anchor
On that rooftop,
Knowing you again.

*

On a practical note, please do not forget to renew your subscriptions (being managed now in-house), and encourage friends to subscribe.

The next double World War 1 issue promises to be very special. Contributions are still being accepted for this (poetry and essays). A general anthology of new poems will be lined up for the New Year of 2015.

Patricia McCarthy

9

Richard Berengarten

Thinking of Sebastian

I first met Sebastian in Cambridge in the mid-1970s thanks to Marie Battle Singer, who was one of my staunchest local supporters when I was founding and setting up the first Cambridge Poetry Festival in 1975. Marie, a New Yorker, was a Freudian analyst and widow of the Scottish poet, James-Burns-Singer. She had a tiny terraced house in Little St. Mary's Lane, where she used to hold literary evenings in her upstairs sitting room. These were cheerful occasions, full of cross-talk and banter. I remember Sebastian vividly as a fine conversationalist and bon viveur. Wearing a black leather jacket, he looked cool, or as we would have said then, smooth.

Sebastian's ideas interested me particularly because he was familiar with both literary and scientific discourses. He had taken a degree in natural sciences at Oxford, followed by an M.A. at UEA, perhaps partly in reaction to the Leavis–Snow 'Two Cultures' controversy of 1962. One of my mentors in the early 1960s, Peter Russell, had always emphasised the need for poets to understand science and keep up with contemporary scientific theories and discoveries.[1] In this respect, Peter followed Hugh MacDiarmid. So, interest in science and insistence that poetry be intelligently involved in the world of ideas formed ground which Sebastian and I shared. Another common interest was in the long poem or sequence, again following the models of poets like Pound, MacDiarmid, Russell and W. S. Graham. For these reasons, I thought of Sebastian as an ally and fellow spirit. Between 1975 and 1985, I think he must have appeared several times at the Cambridge Poetry Festival.

In 1987, keen to get away from Thatcherian Britain and what I saw then, and still see, as the stifling of diversity by a poetry establishment as insular as it is dull, I went to live in Yugoslavia. That meant that I didn't follow or know much about Sebastian's chairmanship of the Poetry Society between 1988 and 1992. My attentions at that time were elsewhere; and for the next twelve years or so, he and I weren't closely in touch, even after my return to England in 1991. During the next decade, for various reasons of my own, I preferred to have as little to do with English poetry circles as possible, especially in London.

Sebastian and I re-established regular contact in 2002 when I learned that

---

[1] Peter Russell, incidentally, edited *Nine* in the late 1950s. He was also a mentor to William Cookson, who founded *Agenda* to continue the Poundian poetics Peter had advocated in *Nine*. I lived in Peter's apartment in Castello, Venice, in 1965-1966.

he had been appointed editor of *The London Magazine*, with which I already had associations in the 1960s, when the editor, Alan Ross, had published several pieces of mine. Now I discovered that Sebastian was keenly interested in my long poem, *The Manager*, which had just appeared. He commissioned a review of it by Angus Calder[2] and included poems of mine in four other issues. So I now had the chance to experience and benefit from Sebastian's critical and selective abilities. As an editor, he was clear-sighted and discerning: firm though courteous in rejecting material, in his acceptances and advocacies he could be positive to the point of passionate enthusiasm. At that time, I also began to understand that Sebastian was no mean strategist in literary politics. Always independent of groups and schools, he knew how to mark out his paths and to line his predilections carefully and caringly, never compromising his own integrity or aligning with groups or schools, whether out of convenience, hope of cosiness, or intellectual cowardice. During this time, we met socially a little more often, including at his house in Stamford Hill, and Melanie and I began to get to know Sebastian's wife Hilary Davies and to appreciate the qualities of her poetry too.

In 2005, Sebastian brought out an extraordinary book entitled *The Matter of Europe*. Published by Anthony Rudolf's Menard Press, this work refuses to fit itself neatly into any single conventional category (poetry, politics, theology, philosophy, history), because it belongs to all of them. The book possesses visionary qualities reminiscent of Blake and Swedenborg. Underlying it is a coherent and inclusive vision of redemption across history, through poetry. History seems to spread out, spatially as it were, as if on a map, as it does in Eliot's 'Burnt Norton'. I recognised at the time that underpinning this book were deep and wide-ranging drillings into European philosophy and theology. What I didn't know, though, and only gradually realised later, was that Sebastian had undergone a conversion to Catholicism. I know now that Hilary's beliefs influenced him in this direction.

In late summer 2013, I contacted Sebastian to ask if he would write a cover-blurb for my forthcoming book of 'metaphysical' sonnets, entitled *Notness*, mainly because he had published several of these in *The London Magazine*. We spoke on the phone: Yes, of course, he said, but added the quiet bombshell, delivered as if as an afterthought, that he had lung cancer and not much time left. A shock, but we went on talking. He very quickly sent a paragraph of commendation for my book: it was to the point and brimful of generosity. Then in November, a printed invitation came to attend the launch

---

[2] *The Manager,* first edition, Elliot and Thompson, London 2001. Angus Calder, 'A Spectacular Variety of Registers', *The London Magazine*, Jan. 2004, pp. 88-95.

of his two new books, *The Land of Gold* and *A Monastery of Light*[3], at St. Paul's School for Girls, an event arranged by Hilary, who had recently retired from her post of Head of Modern Languages there.

I took the train down from Cambridge. In the school's Old Library, Sebastian sat in a wheelchair, greeting everyone attentively, warmly, and affectionately. There was what I can only describe as a statuesque quality about him. Hilary opened a short reading with an impeccably tactful introduction. Sebastian's voice was not strong and he didn't read for long as he was finding breathing difficult. But when he did read, his voice, though gravelly, echoed out sonorous and deep, and everyone present knew that we were in the presence of a Master. The poems from *The Land of Gold* are mainly rhymed quatrains or couplets, with the purity and visionary qualities of *Songs of Innocence and Experience*. The landscape celebrated throughout the open verset structures of *A Monastery of Light* is that of Greece, and in particular, that of the village of Sitohori in the Peloponnese, and its surrounding area, where Sebastian had bought a tumbledown house in 1983, and restored it stone by stone. The prevailing literary influence here is Odysseus Elytis. I responded strongly to both sets of poems. In my own case, the Greek pieces struck an intimate chord: I had myself lived in Greece in the 1960s, and much of my writing is strongly influenced by 20th century Greek poets. Luckily I took a recording of the St. Paul's reading on my pocket dictaphone. After the purity and power of Sebastian's delivery, supported by Hilary's clear voice, I found it impossible to get involved in literary chit-chat and took an earlier train home than I had intended.

Meanwhile, I had been talking to Paul Dominiak, Chaplain at Trinity College, Cambridge, about his continuing the series of poetry readings in the chapel, which he had put on in the previous year under the loose theme of 'poetry and spirituality'. I had mentioned Sebastian's work to him in the summer of 2013. In December, I confirmed with Sebastian and Paul that they were both keen for a reading to take place. So we put it together quickly in the first weeks of January. Hilary and Sebastian chose poems to read out of the two latest books; we agreed that Paul Dominiak and I would introduce it; and Sebastian, Hilary, Clive Wilmer and I would each read some poems, dividing the reading according to Sebastian's preferences. Hilary, Clive and I settled all these details by email.

This event, the last reading Sebastian ever gave, took place in Trinity Chapel on Wednesday 29th January. We knew all along that something special was going on even in preparation. On the evening itself, the audience was

---

[3] *The Land of Gold,* London: Enitharmon Press, 2103; *A Monastery of Light*, London: The Bow-Wow Shop, ed. Michael Glover, 2013.

spellbound. In retrospect, I put this down to four combined factors. First, we all knew that Sebastian was dying and that, as a tribute and celebration, this reading was important; so we entered the situation with a particular sense that combined attentiveness to detail with a quietly controlled poignancy. Second, both books, against all the odds, and in the face of mortality, are filled with celebration, light and love. Third, Sebastian's own presence, despite his physical fragility, was even more statuesque than at St. Paul's, as if he were possessed of a quality of monumentality, resilience and solidity that defied time. Finally, as far as spoken delivery was concerned, while Clive, Hilary and I are all experienced readers, when Sebastian himself read, something else happened. A sonority, authority and dignity emanated from him that set the ears ringing, the spine tingling, the heart speeding, the mind dancing. Everyone present in the audience recognised his depth, authenticity, authority.

After the reading, questions followed, all of which Sebastian answered jovially and wittily. Then a group of friends and family went to a busy restaurant nearby for a celebratory dinner. Sebastian sat halfway along a table, with Hilary beside him and opposite his three daughters, Chloe, Miranda and Xanthi, who had come specially to Cambridge to be present at their dad's reading. He addressed them affectionately as his 'Three Graces'. It was a happy and relaxed evening, full of good conversation and lightened by wines. Sebastian was very fully alive and on the best of form. When Melanie and I said goodbye, he and Hilary were still talking to Clive.

Over the next two days, I forwarded to Hilary the many messages of thanks, praise and congratulation to Sebastian that kept coming into my email box from friends who had been at the reading. In response to one of my messages, sent at 12:25 p.m. on Friday 31st January, Hilary sent me a two-line email at 12:37 p.m. which said that the event had been all the more precious because Sebastian had died suddenly that morning of a cardiac arrest. She added that his last two days had been 'wonderful'.

It is still too soon for the mourning period to have passed. Those of us who knew Sebastian are still filled with all the complex emotions, thoughts and memories that the word 'grief' gathers, though so painfully ineffectively and inadequately. But even now, despite the sadness and sorrow, whenever I think of Sebastian, the total synaesthetic image that comes to my mind – and the image that I know will always appear whenever I think of him in future – is that statuesque presence of his at his last two readings, and above all the sound of his deep voice yielding itself to the rhythms of 'The Ballad of True Regret': 'Gone are the many moments / Like snowflakes into a hand. / Gone are the blissful, intimate scents / Of love in a vanished land.'

And so Sebastian went out in a blaze of love and light and joy and poetry.

Richard Berengarten: Two Elegies

Light fills and fails

In memory of Sebastian Barker

Light fills and fails. It hovers, spills away.
Dark narrows path and yard. Night smothers field.
How foil this overflow? How stall the day?

Out there, against the cliffs, beyond the bay,
a ship is sinking, caving in, unkeeled.
Light fills and fails. It hovers, spills away.

The mast has split in two beneath salt spray,
crushed like an egg, it sinks. Its sides must yield.
How foil this overflow? How stall the day?

No hoop of faith or stave of hope can stay
the chaos that this dark flood has unsealed.
Light fills and fails. It hovers, spills away.

This ground itself unhinges. Rock, mud, clay
swirl as vast spools of shadow are unreeled.
How foil this overflow? How stall the day?

Terror has been unleashed. We're easy prey
to swirling hordes of phantoms day concealed.
Light fills and fails. It hovers, spills away.
How foil this overflow? How stall the day?

The force that fills and empties

In memory of Sebastian Barker

The force that fills and empties things of day
and straddles stars with particles and waves,
holds all our love, yet wipes that love away.

See, night's obsidian floors in rich array
lie strewn with light. Each single one engraves
the force that fills and empties things of day.

Stirring breath, blood and bones, it spurs my clay
to build the buttresses and architraves
that hold our love, but wipes it clean away.

While all things pass, and children run and play,
each atom matter holds connected paves
the force that fills and empties things of day.

Staining the sky in blue, and the blue bay,
sifting clear waters into rills and caves,
it holds our love, yet wipes that love away.

Come, friend, sit with me. Drink this wine, I pray,
and break bread, though around us chaos raves.
The force that fills and empties things of day
holds all our love, yet wipes that love away.

David Cooke

Exile Returning: The Poetry of Harry Clifton

The Winter Sleep of Captain Lemass, (Bloodaxe, 2012)
The Holding Centre, Selected Poems 1974-2004, (Bloodaxe, 2014)

Born in Dublin in 1952, Harry Clifton is a contemporary of such luminaries as Paul Muldoon, Tom Paulin and Ciaran Carson, and, like them, started publishing his earliest poems in *The Honest Ulsterman* during the darkest days of The Troubles. Like theirs, his was a precocious talent which led to him publishing two collections, *The Walls of Carthage* (1977) and *The Office of the Salt Merchant* (1979), both with The Gallery Press, while still in his twenties. However, even now, it is unlikely that his name is as well known as theirs on this side of the water; while even in Ireland recognition was slow in coming. One reason for this, no doubt, was that Clifton, like his fellow Dubliners Joyce and Beckett, spent many years abroad. In fact, there can be few major poets who have travelled as widely or worked as variously as Clifton in West Africa, Thailand, Germany, Italy and France, until his final return to Ireland in 2004. It was at this point that his position as one of the country's finest poets was established when he won the *Irish Times* Poetry Now Award for his monumental *Secular Eden, Paris Notebooks 1994-2004*. Then, in 2010 his status was reaffirmed when he was appointed Ireland's Professor of Poetry. Recently published by Bloodaxe, his latest collection is *The Winter Sleep of Captain Lemass*. However, with the publication of *The Holding Centre, Selected Poems 1974-2004,* there is a long overdue opportunity for new readers to discover the full range of his work in a judicious sampling of poems that goes back three decades.

On the periphery of the Irish and British poetry scenes throughout his formative years, Clifton's chances of establishing his poetic credentials in the UK were probably also hampered by his Southern Irish provenance at a time when the media spotlight was firmly focused on poetry from the North. However, this may well have given Clifton the freedom to go his own way when others, such as Muldoon, Mahon and Heaney, were reacting impatiently to demands that they should be 'responding' in some obvious way to their political 'situation'. Heaney, the leader of the pack, famously summed up his attitude in 'Whatever You Say Say Nothing', which he wrote 'after an encounter / With an English journalist in search of 'views / on the Irish thing.' Although throughout those years poets in the North did of course respond, each in their own way and with varying degrees of directness or obliquity, to what Joyce famously called 'the nightmare of history', it is probably Tom Paulin who is most like Clifton in his tendency to confront head on the facts of history and politics. Moreover, although Clifton's trajectory as a writer starts in Ireland – and his own family history has not been left unscarred by its politics – the scope of his poems is such that the Irish 'Troubles' might, to quote from Patrick Kavanagh's poem 'Epic', seem merely 'a local row'.

Turning now to the poems, what strikes one immediately, is how technically proficient Clifton was, even in his early twenties, and how immediately recognizable his voice was. There was already a confessional directness, a vulnerability that seemed a world away from the whimsicality and exuberance of his close contemporary Paul Muldoon. 'Blue', one of his many cityscapes, captures the mundane reality of a Dublin morning, while at the same time hinting at personal dissatisfaction: 'Your mind is plunged / In the wrong kind of work ... Work dissolves in legitimate failure.' Moreover, one senses, perhaps, behind the poem's opening stanza a hint of Pascal's *le silence eternel de ces espaces infinis*:

One day, you wake
Conscious of blue space
In which a pure sun has been blazing
For hours, while innocent trees
Perfect themselves invisibly
Just outside.
        Ethereal,
Neither near nor far,
The city is a grey rumour.

'The North Wall', another poem set in Dublin, casts a cold eye upon Irish commercial aspirations long before the myth of the Celtic Tiger: 'Some men estimate their souls / At six red tractors, or a gross / of skins on the back board of a lorry ... // Some men's pledges go with the tides.' It is always tempting for the intellectual to condemn the bourgeoisie and to be dismissive of enterprise. Nevertheless, there are always winners and losers. 'The Blue Room' is an effective early portrayal of some unemployed men playing billiards:

Five o'clock passes, half-five. Big time avarice
Has paid off its losers. But these play on,
Who have no stake in that more loaded game.

In the light of Ireland's recent economic meltdown, this is a poem which might now seem prophetic, or merely a latter day expression of Yeats' contempt for 'the greasy till'. However, beyond mere 'boom and bust' it could be argued that the revelations of corruption at the heart of the Catholic Church will have a far more lasting effect upon the fabric of Irish society. The title poem of Clifton's first collection, *The Walls of Carthage,* gives more than a hint of what was to come. Set against the backdrop of St Augustine's asceticism and the Church's insistence upon celibacy, Clifton voices the frustrations of a middle aged priest: 'Oases of discontent, // Paris, Maynooth, Louvain, / define my forty year desert, / Home from home, terrain / Of groundless visions.'

Having established some of his main themes from the outset, we find Clifton, in subsequent volumes, revisiting them in the course of his wide-ranging travels. *The Office of the Salt Merchant* contains several impressive poems set in West Africa that show the extent to which Clifton's work matured in the two years following his début. 'The Desert Route', packed with brilliantly observed details, has the immediacy of reportage:

> Exempted from living, abandoned
> To some infinite fascination he has
> With a gentle goat by a wall,
> Here where the trade routes start
>
> The idiot sits, clad in the cast-offs
> Of a town full of tailors,
> Unembarrassed
> By any such thing as self.

The poem's Audenesque conclusion evokes, with a few deft strokes, a border control, 'where a soldier / with three stripes, wishing himself elsewhere, / is waving the landrovers on'. Equally memorable are 'Government Quarters', 'Niger Ferry' or 'Latitude 5° N', which is based on Clifton's experiences as a teacher in a missionary school. With its four capacious stanzas, it is a brilliant distillation of febrile chaos in postcolonial Africa. In *Comparative Lives* (1982) there are poems such as 'Michael Praetorius' and 'The Family Bass' in which protagonists struggle to shake off the twin burdens of 'family and politics – lost causes' However, it is at this point that Clifton's travels take him to south-east Asia in the aftermath of the Vietnam War and the genocide of the Khmer Rouge. First published in the *New Statesman* by Derek Mahon, always an advocate of Clifton's work, 'Monsoon Girl' is a frank avowal of sexuality and loneliness in the Tropics.

Your nudity dapples the walls
With shadows, and splashes the mirrors
Like a vision, in the blue light
That bathes you, a pleasure-girl
On a lost planet, sincere
But only at night.

Powerful, too, is 'Death of Thomas Merton'. Characterized by the poet as 'one of the Catholic great', Merton was a Trappist monk. He was also a charismatic and eclectic visionary, who died in Bangkok in 1968. Written in the ample stanzas that have increasingly become one of Clifton's signature forms, the poem opens on a note of disillusion: 'Losing altitude, you see below you the flames / Of the Tet offensive, giving the lie to your visions / Of Eastern mystics'.

Throughout the 1980s and early 1990s Clifton's work went from strength to strength, his lens scanning both *Mitteleuropa* after the collapse of communism and the Fascist inheritance of Italy. In 'Exiles' we find him married, but restless as ever, pondering upon the meaning of 'home' and coming to another Audenesque conclusion that 'the blur of cities / Is one city, simultaneous, / Eternal, from which we are exiled forever.' In his broodingly discursive meditation, 'At the Grave of Silone', he finds himself praying at 'the shrine of ordinariness' and comes to the conclusion: '*Fontamara*... it could have been / Aranyaprathet, or Ballaghadereen.'

Published in 1994, *Night Train Through The Brenner* was to be Clifton's last collection until *Secular Eden, Paris Notebooks 1994-2004* was published in the United States by Wake Forest University Press thirteen years later.

Two hundred pages long and containing more than a hundred poems, it is an overwhelming body of work, whose impact as been alluded to above. It's a volume which anyone interested in Clifton's work should read. Viewing it as a series of five 'notebooks' may well seem appropriate, given the existential slant of Clifton's work and his ongoing quest to free himself from the Joycean 'nightmare'. However, it should not suggest that there is anything extempore or merely provisional about the writing it contains, beyond a certain unevenness which is, perhaps, inevitable in a collection of such amplitude. Its magnificent opening poem, 'When the Promised Day Arrives', takes as its starting point a journey through city streets: 'urban trains, their clean electric smell... Fish and vegetable stalls, a splash of awnings ...The sizzle of meat/ on skillets, chantilly and rum/ in sawdust joints'. However, in his collection's title poem he moves beyond journalistic facility to explore what it means to be human:

Six o'clock in secular Eden –
No one will ever fall from grace
Where the bells are electric, and the chimes
Of a French municipal hall
Preserve us in time.

Clifton's insistence that all values are human and that we only have one life
is handled most daringly in, 'God in France', where even the deity has given
up on his traditional role and yearns to 'to live again in the body', leaving in
the lurch those communities who kill each other and invoke him by different
names. Its closing lines are impressive:

Let judgment take care of itself. To celebrate –
That was the one imperative. Randomness, flux,
Drew themselves about me as I ate,
Protected by the nearness of women, their sex
Blown sheer through summer dresses, loving my food,
My freedom, as they say a man should.

Elsewhere, he again conveys his uneasy relationship with Ireland in
several poems inspired by occasional return visits. In 'The Country of Still
Waters' the protagonist comes back to 'an old stone house, a mother and two
daughters/laying the same ghost, unweaving the hex/like retted flax.' The
near normality of sectarian hatred is evoked in 'The Black Book' where 'the
executioners' are 'doing time/ In the open prisons of their own kitchens, /
Reminiscing, over hot strong cups of tea.' In 'Icy Pandemonium' the contrast
between the ancestral home and the life he has made for himself abroad is
made explicit:

Suspended in mid-flight,
I dream of a bare table, the warmth to come,
A silence at the heart of Paris, a room,
Detached, anonymous, nothing to do but write.

However, it is in *The Winter Sleep of Captain Lemass* that he explores most
thoroughly his conflicted relationship with the land of his birth. Here is his
untitled prefatory sonnet:

Dublin under sea-fog, dreeping weather,
Salt air blown inland…The cab turns west
At Brady's pharmacy, into the nightlit drizzle

Of Harrington Street. And now for the acid test –
Alive to the danger in this monkey-puzzle
Of Ancestry, this maze of one-way streets,
Are you not scared, young man, of your Daddy's ghost
And his before him, waiting here to greet you,
Latest of blow-ins, ready to try again?

Unlike Joyce and Beckett who never came back, it seems that Clifton has now at last returned to face to his demons. Nowhere is this expressed more powerfully than in his title poem, where he evokes the notorious killing of Captain Noel Lemass, the brother of Sean Lemass, the foremost statesman of Ireland in the 1960s, with whom Clifton has family ties. Fighting on the Republican side in the Irish Civil War, Noel Lemass was taken away to be executed or murdered, call it what you will, by 'free staters' in 1923, after the signing of the Anglo-Irish Treaty in 1921 and the establishment of The Irish Free State in 1922: 'Your eyes. Blindfolded, beheld the ideal State / As the real one steadied itself / To annihilate you.' In the poem's second section '1943' a female presence is evoked whose reminiscences may, it is hoped, 'shed a little more light … on our bitterness, our confusion.' Appalled by the internecine conflict that has scarred Irish history, Clifton is equally scathing about contemporary Ireland. In 'The Crystalline Heaven' he imagines himself as Dante looking down 'on the dog-eat-dog of Florence, or Dublin town' and sets the tone with an epigraph from the Inferno: 'The new people, the quick money'. In this poem the concentric seats of Dáil Eireann seem a parody of the 'concentric hells' of Dante's great poem. Evoking the corrupt figure of Charlie Haughey, Ireland's prime minister in the 1980s, Clifton hints at future economic woes: 'Let Charlie soon start shiting golden eggs / Or the country's fucked.' Quoting Yeats, he highlights the contrast between Ireland's revolutionary past and the sleaziness that has replaced it:

Charlie Haughey crosses the floor,
Engages a woman I know in conversation –
Still beautiful, still a gazelle. After how many years
Of marriage to a Dublin auctioneer?

In this collection, as in its predecessors, Clifton gives short shrift to Ireland's institutionalized Catholicism with its tradition of guilt and sexual hypocrisy. In 'Skellig Michael' he describes the rock that is a monument to Ireland's monastic tradition and debunks the so called 'golden age' when Ireland was 'a land of saints and scholars':

No, as the engine stops
And the pilgrims stuffed with Quells
In the oily swell,

The guilty, the inadequate,
Each with his middle-aged dread,
Are lifted up, and grimly swung ashore,
I feel I have been here, in my head,
Too many times before.

The Winter Sleep of Captain Lemass is an austere and unrelenting work and although, superficially, the titles of some poems such as 'Toome' or 'Eels' may be reminiscent of Heaney, Clifton has none of the older poet's warmth or his sense of identity with a community, so that if one has to make a criticism it would be that, ultimately, the vision is perhaps just a shade too bleak and unrelieved. Nevertheless, this is the work of an ambitious poet of real stature. Like Swift and Juvenal, Clifton excoriates sleaze and hypocrisy. Like Beckett and Baudelaire, he is a connoisseur of ennui. It is to be hoped that the publication of his two most recent volumes by the ever-enterprising Bloodaxe Books will gain for him that wider UK readership he so clearly deserves.

Simon Jenner

A Secretary of Hidden Powers: The Poetry of Robert Nye

Robert Nye (1939) has been called one of the truest and purest poetic voices of his generation, or subsequently. The Cholmondeley Award he received in 2007 was more cleanly and less automatically earned than has sometimes been the case.

He determinedly avoids the mainstream, wrote acclaimed novels for over 30 years like *Falstaff* (1976), and *The Voyage of the Destiny* (1982) and *The Late Mr Shakespeare* (1998), his final novel. But his calling and core excellence has always been poetry, which is recognized, too quietly for media or poetry scene attention. This is partly his fault: he lives semi-reclusively in Ireland, and has been a very successful novelist yet retired from that; has written just criticism, is known for humbling scholars in debate. Four things to damn him by the mainstream, for a few years, perhaps.

Nye's *Collected Poems* came out several times, but the latest edition, *The Rain and the Glass* a *New and Selected* with his incessant felicitous revisions, dates from 2005. His subsequent collection *An Almost Dancer* (Greenwich Exchange, 2012) draws on nearly all – but irritatingly not all – the poems he has published since. The omissions can be remedied by recourse to the TLS, and is a small blemish. It seems publisher James Hodgson objected to the lubricity of some of Nye's recent poems, although the TLS had seen fit to publish them. Hodgson, editor as well as publisher, is a fine 1890s scholar and it's a startling misjudgement he has probably already regretted; and to be remedied I trust in a later *Collected Poems*. This selection does however usefully collect critical garlands of nearly two pages at the back, which positions Nye for new readers. And it gathers nearly all of Nye's poems since 2005. Here is the title poem:

An Almost Dancer

Once, on a hill in Wales, one summer's day
I almost danced for what I thought was joy.

An hour or more I'd lain there on my back
Watching the clouds as I gazed dreaming up.

As I lay there I heard a skylark sing
A song so sweet it touched the edge of pain.

I dreamt my hair was one with all the leaves
And that my legs sent shoots into the earth.

Laughing awake, I lay there in the sun
And knew that there was nothing to be known.

Small wonder then that when I stood upright
I felt like dancing. Oh, I almost danced,

I almost danced for joy, I almost did.
But some do not, and there's an end of it.

One night no doubt I shall lie down for good
And when I do perhaps I'll dance at last.

Meanwhile I keep this memory of that day
I was an almost dancer, once, in Wales.

This is typically epiphanic and as typically wry. The title naturally warns us but the adjectival caution doesn't detract from the headlong nature of the noun. There's some affinity with David Gascoyne's early 'Poem' of 1933, though without its angst around 'the threshold of vertiginous summer' where 'I flung this foursquare body down'. The affinities persist but attest curiously to the fact that Nye has been doing rather more of this than Gascoyne ever did. It's typical too that the magical narrative leads into the quotidian fact of – however magically endowed – 'some do not' as Ford Madox Ford also said and 'there's an end of it.' It isn't, of course, since Nye invokes an afterlife of possibilities, including dance. The poem sashays its way through naturalism, magical assertion, blunt personal limitation, and possible transcendent resurrection. The wryness is all. You believe him; or you ought to.

As Andrew McCulloch in the *TLS* has suggested about this poem, Shelley holds no monopoly on skylarks. McCulloch also attests to G. S. Fraser's praise of the young Nye's leaning into a poem, his being a 'secretary of hidden powers ... nothing demands more delicate and conscious shaping than a true lyrical poem'. Nye's truest (if occasionally gruff) reader was his old friend Martin Seymour-Smith, who confirmed for Nye – when the latter was just sixteen – the lyric spareness he was born with was a true gift, and introduced him to Robert Graves and (vicariously) Laura Riding, with different results, but who themselves also reinforced Nye's refusal to reach for afflatus: post-romantic or post-Movement ration book, unwieldy metaphor, or anything but the spareness differently honoured by each. Here

24

is the opening of Nye's elegy for Seymour-Smith, 'Valentinus':

> Yes, I knew Valentinus from my youth.
> He taught me poets have to tell the truth
> Or try to, though it make us seem uncouth.
>
> You find this foolish? Lady, so did he,
> Laughing at his own verses, teaching me
> To laugh at mine or simply let them be.
>
> Not that it's ever simple to make sense
> At least when living in the present tense,
> Or to be more than your intelligence.

This recalls not only Nye's but – for those who knew and now read him – Seymour-Smith's precise talk. The admonition 'to be more than your intelligence' is something clearly apprehended if elusive. It recalls too Seymour-Smith's praise for fusion of sensibility with intelligence (and the poem ends with tears of recognition), but also for that listening out, the by-passing of intelligence to find it in lyric forms not answerable in straight prose. Nye layers his audience with a veneer-maker's economy. He genders the interlocutor, lending her an unwonted patina of Donnean dust: though doubtless some poets still 'lady' their addressees, the effect is deliberately positioning epochs. The title suggests some 17th century soubriquet, and Seymour-Smith's Renaissance Man scholarship in so many epochs isn't in doubt.

ii

Nye's scholarship is something he wears lightly and almost denies. In fact he refracts it through smelly ghosts and the imagination to produce such snotty-nosed gems as these:

> I've never seen the ghost of Chatterton
> But sometimes I have smelt it, sharp as day:
> A scent half smegma and half innocence
> Like the stale-almond sweetness of the may.

Another fragrance might be Seymour-Smith's stale pipe and sweetness of single Speyside. He was a bantam-weight boxing champion in the army, and one is tempted to suggest he obliquely turns up as Keats (they were of a height). This is 'The Knock-Out'; where Cowden Clarke recalls his old pupil John Keats reliving with relish his own encounter of a boxing match: 'the champion drops / But first he spins, eyes rolling in a swoon / Of sweet obliteration', ending

> His nightingale sings on of course, but I
> Prefer remembering his commentary
> On that young boxer's quick three punches, plain
> Poetry as his fingers tap the pane.

Cowden Clarke always talked up the 'manly' Keats to counterblast Shelley's 'Adonais', and Nye's poem captures Regency speech and the narrator. There are wholly different sporting memories in 'The Gambler' about his father's passing on the horse-betting gene to his son who was known for it. The variety and pitch of the volume is greater perhaps than any of Nye's previous collections encapsulating memory, childhood, art, death, dead poets and dead horses, bees and poets and indeed eroticism as major themes. At which point poems placed on Hodgson's Pater-wracked codex should at least be mentioned. Here's the opening of 'The Guitar Lesson' subtitled 'After Balthus':

> The girl lies stretched out on her teacher's lap
> Herself the instrument for playing now,
> Her frock rucked up, her knickers off, one hand
> Flailing the floor beside the brittle strings
> She has abandoned for this ecstasy
> Of music-making in a secret room
> Where none can see or hear them except us.

The disturbed image of Balthus, controversial enough, has not invited many interpreters from the 'After' school of polite paintings poets (they painlessly swerved Kingsley Amis's blast at them in the fifties). It's too disturbing for nervous deconstructive liberals too. Nye is more cunning in his empathy, moving through the painting to the subject, the painter and the girl portrayed (not the same as the subject at all). It begins in depicting Balthus as Balthus might have wished to depict himself; it ends though:

> Balthus confessed it smelt of sulphur,
> This scene from the inferno of desire
> And yet in painting it his inspiration
> Seems to have been a quattrocento pieta,
> Which makes his girl guitar a kind of Christ.

Conspiring with the real, so Artaud said,
He uses sex to crucify us better.

But what about the girl? Such metaphysics
Leaves out of all account her mortal look.
Her eyes are almost shut, her lips just open
As if to cry for mercy or dispatch.
What she might say should be our only theme
Who gaze upon her as the woman does
With the half-smile of Bluebeard in his rage.

This reminds us that narrative as well as lyric is in Nye's gift and that one of his novels was *Gilles de Rais* (1990). The movement from sex as neo-paedophilic voyeurism to meta-sex and existential suffering is exquisite and seamlessly wrought. Nye packs in a wide scholarship without pedantry or losing his unease or uneasy itch. It's the sort of thing one finds in his novels but pitched to a jittery sublimity. No-one else would have dared essay this theme, let alone lead it through such insight without descending into tittering pornography or stepped back into appalled self-judgement – which Nye also gets in without slipping off the blues of his own guitar.

Nye's voice as such has – without recourse to iron-wrought syntax or glacial patterns of narrative – changed less over the years than many contemporaries. What has changed is the listener in the act of listening; the time-wrought shudder that first lashes then remorsefully leaves the poet. Nye's attention to the natural world is clear, but the act of listening as one ages, the joke on oneself, is clearer with each collection.

iii

Nye's exact knowledge of Shakespeare's London or the natural world is pared down to a verbal simplicity that is pellucid, haunted and holds attention because of the power in its economy. His final novel *The Late Mr Shakespeare* boasts a central character Pickleherring, a boy actor for Shakespeare, now writing a fire is about to engulf London in 1666. So 'Request', the last poem in the collection, revisits Nye's boy and man hero and omega self:

… It's where I lived
When I was nearly happy, years ago.
I beg you, sir, for the sweet love of Christ,
Tell me the way to Pickle Herring Street.

Much has been written about such economy, about such paring-away, in the modernist (Ungaretti, Celan) or post-modern sense, that now pervades poetry workshops. Doubtless useful. But when confronting a Nye poem, such commentaries become a little more meaningless.

The paring away in this collection holds that valedictory charge one finds quietly blazing in volumes proclaimed as final, and this Nye suggests will be his last, after debilitating illness. At the comparatively young age of 73 Nye it is hoped will be proved wrong. So to begin with endings (the last written of these poems) 'Instructions for a Burial' Nye commences:

> Bury me in a rut on Clay Pit Hill
> In a cardboard box to let the worms in quick

But of course a rut is not where Nye ends, even if his body does:

> A few peewits as mourners would be good
> But if they have some better thing to do
> Then I forgive them, as I now forgive
> All those who trespass against me and tramp
> Over the queer grave where my corpse decays
> Stuck on a rut on top of Clay Pit Hill.

Still more moving is another self-explanatory poem, 'In Still Winter':

> Now at the edge of consciousness
> I could believe that more or less
> Each babe's that's born, from its first cry,
> Is God demanding, 'Who am I?'
> Though some men, dying, ask the same,
> And cry to Christ for why they came.

Transcendence needn't be so painful. Nye is a comic novelist, though it's a pretty transcendent comedy he invokes. Comedy grounds it. Nye would endorse T. E. Hulme's now anachronistic 'I shall call my book Valet to the Absolute: the absolute not a hero to his own valet.' This divined comedy in the broadest (not funny, and Dante comes into it) sense erupts most in 'Bicycling with Birds', 'Mentchikoffs', 'In Still Winter' and in the title poem. As James Aitchison notes in the *London Magazine,* 'Drinking Hot Chocolate in the Rain' starts in a cardboard cup and soars:

> There in the market by the coffee-stall
> I saw the world turned inside-out. The rain

28

Flew upwards like so many crystal sparks
Returning to the glory of the sun
As I drank my dark chocolate to the dregs.

This, this is ecstasy, to stand and drink
Hot chocolate in the rain, lost in a crowd
Of strangers, and to feel for them such love
As Dante felt for Beatrice when he saw
Her passing by and own heart bowed down.

iv

In a way the novelist Nye might appreciate, it's worth at this point just briefly signposting why Nye has been read so keenly by poets for nearly sixty years. Admirable short epigrammatic poems read themselves in the earlier *Collected* which might be tracked down first: like 'November Sun', 'An Answer for the Owl', 'Catching Leaves' 'Poppies', 'John Donne and the Candle', 'One or Two Swallows', 'All Hallows', 'No Second Sight', 'The Grasshopper', 'Unlikeness', 'That Raven', and the haunting 'A Former House'. That litany suggests range too. Some poems like that last or 'Ropes' are enviably clear, furnishing a metaphoric rightness and finish. 'Listeners' written at thirteen follows a procedure Nye would try elsewhere, but this early piece is a gem to start with. Nye was horribly precocious. He knew too that his beginning prefigured his end: the title of his last quasi-Collected was a line from that very poem: 'The Rain and the Glass'.

Several poems like 'Poppies', 'Between', and the superb 'Divisions on a Ground' from his eponymous 1976 collection, and 'Otherwise Elsewhere', are far knottier than most others; which take on some of the toughness one associates almost with Laura Riding or mid-Graves, different to either in their warmth. This is rare in that sense, since Nye has a far greater generosity than Laura Riding whom he knew, and doesn't inhabit that pure conceptualising surface that Riding, or, supremely, Dickinson manage. But Nye tends to approach such states through stalking metaphors, as in such recent poems as 'The Task' and 'The Prize' with their obsessive teasing out of what fable constitutes poetry. 'Hares Dancing' with its Herrickian rhythm and simplicity inhabits the same valedictory blessing on his world, which is what makes it so right an ending of the 1976 volume, and a disarming to the fashionable:

I will close my eyes
And see no more lies
But dance with the dancing hares.

'The Task' generates a pure narrative metaphor that most probably could never follow through without gnarling it somehow near the trees fronting the house. 'Henry James' and 'Late Victorian Sonnet' are the kind of comic poem one has simply not read for a long time, almost a lost art; like the comic verse of Praed, Calverley, J K Stephen, Graves, Cameron, Drummond Allison for that matter.

'Margaretting' – a place dreamt of that he might invent ('And marry Margaret from Margaretting') – caresses with a lightness of touch that comes from a grace simply extinct these days. 'Raleigh Said' is a curiously powerful, more freighted condensation, prophetic of his novel on the same subject later. An eerily convincing oblique slice on the times; different to much else in his volume. 'Remembering No Name' ends beautifully too. 'Hospital Incident' again drives an incident to its inevitable heart-rending. A dying boy is brought oranges by his mother. He throws one through the window in a final despairing affirmation of his existence, eliciting protests. 'He lies face down in his blood./ How's that ladies? Just once. Pardon him.' Nye's language is less ornate than most, so the details stand out.

His work becomes darker and more subtle, especially with revisions. *Darker Ends* as a volume is very much conceived as a sequence. The middle stanza is full of Jansenist self-questioning, frightening his child with shadow-play:

Why do I scare him? Fearful of my love
I'm cruelly comforted by his warm fear,
Seeing the night made perfect on the wall
In my handwriting, if illegible,
Still full of personal beasts, and terrible.

'Night Watch' is a fine successor to 'Darker Ends' with that layering of dreams-within-dreams and the mirror world of pretending not to sleep. 'Christmas Eve' follows poignantly from that, and 'A Bat in a Box' is a fluttery tour de force. The end ironically is telescoped, and one unravels it slowly. The bat is like a trapped dark heart. 'Dedications', breaks the whole mid-winter child waking sequence in a very adult manner. Recalling inscribed copies of his book to his ex-wife, he ends 'For I loved the girl who read them for their virtue/And now you have my vices and my name.' In this collection one can see the themes developed, like 'A Golden Knot' which seems a tender reprieve from the reproof of the previous poem (which does seem to be addressed to a partner). 'The Stoat' with its later spawn, 'Sign' does elicit a density of response, sexual and displaced freedoms, still there, and the neat epigrammatic set of images sharply set off in 'Signs'.

'Any Other Enemy' is elusive at first, but with Nye one finds a simpler way of reading, that the protagonist might as well have been anyone, including 'any other enemy' which includes the self as hostile (predatory I assume) although a friend; and then the twist of collaboration. 'The Same Song' transparently pursues the same Darker Ends as that title poem, the sensitive man wounding through fear of over-sensitiveness those he loves. Telling is the 'No, music, I've no natural explanations' since the addressee becomes something unexpected, not her, the protagonist self or the reader. Music can be sinned against and was most, here.

'Gone Out' begins with pragmatic displacement: 'Whenever you leave the house I write a poem' and then platonically concludes:

> Yet when you've gone an hour the poem fades...
> Which draws me out to stand and watch the way
> Through the long valley, hoping you'll come back
> To give my words the simple truth they lack.

Not many, recalling Wilde, could get away with that last phrase. It also pre-echoes and now resembles Seymour-Smith's masterpiece 'The Internal Saboteur'. The physicality is always more palpable and almost biblical, suggesting that tradition drawn from poets like Crashaw whom Nye admires. 'At Last' from this time in Nye's life summarises this fear-of-not-loving-truly theme that the mid-to-late 1960s seems to highlight in his work. It's quite an early maturity: Nye's recognizable sonance, his tone was something reached perhaps by twenty four, then pared by the kind of gift that turns in on itself, but doesn't consume its tail. Nye's development's been steadier than many, because clear from the outset. Another title of the 1969 collection, had he not written 'Darker Ends' would be 'An Absence of Nettles'. It recalls Hardy, and Graves when touched by Hardy, but only Nye could have written it. 'I like nettles, but I took /An old scythe for your sake...' ending:

> But now – no flowers have come
> To fit your shadows;
> The earth will not accept
> The seeds you sow. And who can care for
> An absence of nettles, an ungrowing place?

If Nye is thought of a poet's poet, this is just and unjust; but will ensure he rides fashion and outwears it. Some poems will last, as Nye himself said generously of Derek Stanford, as long as the language. Here is another reason from his new collection:

31

Matches

Some matchsticks in a patch of melting tar
Held my attention for at least an hour
One afternoon when I was rising four.
Crouched in the shadow of some willow trees
I stared at them and saw the way love sees,
And all was close and clear and singular.

Three matchsticks in a black hot patch of tar,
One spent, one bent, one still a fusilier
Standing up proud and perpendicular
With fire in his head, my cavalier.
Well, I knelt by them on my naked knees,
Transfixed as always by simplicities.

I loved those lordlings of the molten square,
My puny masters stuck in hot black tar,
Though only now I've worked the reason out
(If love needs reasons, which of course I doubt):
We're outcast in this world, and derelict,
Matches from nothing into nowhere flicked.

John Horder has written: 'The poet laureate Carol Ann Duffy has written in *The Guardian*: 'At his best, his [Robert Nye's] work wears a curious permanence.' Why doesn't she recommend him to receive the Queen's Medal for Poetry? I can only echo that, knowing Nye would laugh to the echo.

Patricia McCarthy

Taking the Mickey

Brendan Kennelly: *Guff* (Bloodaxe, 2014)

Brendan Kennelly's refreshingly vital, entertaining new collection, *Guff*, written with real verve and spirit, is certainly worth noting, coming as it does late in the poet's distinguished career, and containing the same freshness, saucy satire and depths recognisable in the corpus of his work as it tackles major themes. Guff represents the rubbish or crap that we put up with in our materialistic world, the main persona being Everyman and the alter ego of the poet.

Chuckles are never far away as Guff takes the mickey:

> If we forget our jigs and reels
>   we can always jive.

or

> Is there a truth in ignorance?
>   Is education lies?

This startling collection, in which the poems link and accrue with repeated, evolving images, is a bold, Swiftian satire on the way we live our lives: a social commentary, taking the mickey out of the bourgeoisie, the superficial values which surround us in our daily lives. Kennelly's Ireland could be anywhere in our day and age, for it is a cosmos that Kennelly is invoking in this major work. His social satire, savage and politically incisive, concerns an Ireland taken over by the Celtic Tiger. Tigertown is full of 'cunts and pricks', paedophiles, victims, where 'talk of money' is 'Ireland's real religion'. 'Celtic Tiger' even becomes a woman, 'a ravenous bitch' who 'lives on the flesh of the poor'. Of the 'Tiger family' Guff comments, tongue in cheek: 'God bless the Tiger family/ who know that greed is good'

The pervasive wit, irony, aphorisms, iconoclastic belly laughs – 'Consider, then, the power of Art/ that can make a poem out of a fart' – moments of illumination and poignant intimate confessions are part of this heady mix, showing a poet not concerned merely with the lyric, although he is up to the best of the lyricists when he wishes as evidenced here: 'When words melt in music's arms/ Guff's teeshirt is a cloak of charms', in the seagull with its neck 'a white jewel in the sun', swallows whose wings are 'small thunder', such birds as inspire his earlier collections.

Guff is the spokesman for our age. He is an Everyman, a sensitive loner, a lovable, quirky outsider who speaks in the language of the vernacular, using slang, aphorisms and clichés, and languages such as those of the nursery rhyme, the bible, the catechism and of prayer. He isn't even sure what language he speaks: 'I shouldn't be so cheeky/ as to ask the wind what its language is/ when I'm not so sure of my own'. He can be bawdy, sexy, outspoken, touchingly humble and poignant, and downright funny. Through his persona, Kennelly is not afraid to confront politics, terrorism, murderers, religion, alongside the desperation for peace: 'if waves were peace, peace, peace/ let them break over me'; in fact, Guff takes on just about everything in his stream of consciousness. His words might fly 'like hungry birds through his brain' but he is also, between the lines, an erudite mocker of our whole intellectual set-up on this earth:

> Guff saw Descartes in Asdee
> Thinking.
>
> Guff saw Tarzan up a tree.
>
> Guff put two and two together.
> Nothing.
>
> ('The Guff Principle')

Very much in a Kennelly timbre and lingo, at the same time there are echoes in Guff's voice of Vladimir and Estragon from Beckett's *Waiting for Godot*: In the poem 'Zip your lip', Guff concludes: 'there's no need for words/ and words have no need for people'. Words, Guff knows, can even choke you. Even the surrealistic images in *Guff* – such as Guff's idea of Yeats' paradisical island, 'the Isle of Innisfree' which is about to house 'a 22-apartment development' with 'underground parking' and no pollution, and the images Guff gives for himself in 'he felt he was' such as 'a fly in the Ryder Cup,/ a plastic spoon up to its neck in sand/ a blind magpie' attest to the pervasive meaninglessness of contemporary existence, alleviated only, perhaps, as Larkin also mooted – by love, and by surprise moments of illumination or epiphany.

The clever parallel between Guff and Caliban must be deliberate: both are crude and at times rude, yet gifted with articulacy and with redemptive powers. Guff lives in a 'rented cave', 'a deep unprogressive cave' on an island 'in one corner of which/ people kill/ each other' and rapes occur, wives are battered (Guff realises the awful truth of when, maybe out of fear, 'The more savage he is/ the more excuses she makes for him'), where (cynically) 'Poems bloom out of butchered blood'. Guff internalises this island image – 'every man is an island'? – and lives isolated in the 'small corners of his island mind' in which he says he seeks 'to find the little I can find'. He is full of self-disgust – 'I'm allergic to myself', he claims, as throughout the book he scratches himself, underlying a general disgust with the human condition. In the poem, 'Let Guff come coughing', Guff/Caliban (the latter after all was also gifted with articulacy and lyrical speech) chants:

> Let Guff come laughing from his cave
> at the lies of life, truth of the grave.
> Hairy corpses don't need to shave
> but the living must be razorsharp
> before they dance to an angel's harp.

Guff plays unashamedly to the gallery, to all tiers of society, especially to the groundlings, using titbits of local gossip, news, jibing at irrelevances that are magnified into importance via local slang. For example, the humour of the pat rhyme is full of irony in 'When the farmer grows to love the fox/ And Dublin's virgins fit in a box' and in the single line for indigenous Irish who are only too familiar with the rivalry between Dublin and Cork: 'When Dublin and Cork fall deep in love', plus another irresistible couplet, with its dig at the Church:

> When nun and whore, scribbler and vandal
> Taste a breakfast not laced with scandal
> ('An honest man')

In the single line from 'She's gone', 'Where is Sally Noggin gone?' he also plays around wickedly with familiar place names to get his laugh. Sallynoggin is one gigantic concrete estate, certainly once quite a deprived suburb of Dublin.

The world which praises the acquisition of facts by 'those creatures' Guff calls 'other men', when Guff doesn't have a single fact in his head, is also satirised. For example in the poem, 'The extent', Guff concludes: 'The extent of his not knowing/ says "Don't worry how deep the Shannon is./ It's flowing". The rhyming of the 'ing' sounds symbolise amusingly how he is comforting himself with this, and simultaneously mocking factual people for their limitations.

Language is a dominant theme. Guff is very aware of words, and stories, including the silences behind them. Language itself it like a living creature:

> Guff reads a book of bad blood
> The book of bad blood reads Guff
> He doesn't like being read by a book
> ('bad blood')

The words have a life of their own. They are his ally but also his enemy. For example when Guff is trying to write a letter with something 'throttling him', 'The words mock him after two sentences./ They sneer at him, their eyes cruel with ridicule./ They form a jibing chorus'.

He even makes up his own language such as 'gigglemocked', 'slickscissored', 'seasmile', 'witchtit'. At times he can't find the right words, feels stymied e.g. in trying to praise the water for all its 'cleaning' including of the 'filth of woman and man', he can't make himself 'happy' by finding even one line:

> but I can't, I can't
>   not one line
> not a single line of praise
>   that might justify
> my foolish ruminating days.

In moments like these, 'When his heart, like the world/ is witchtit dry' and 'When water drips in his mind like/ Chinese torture', he resorts to comfort-eating five Bewley's buns!

Not much misses Guff's seemingly naïve but scathing eye or mind. Stories as a theme run through the sequence. Maybe the true stories remain unspoken. As Guff, surely Kennelly's alter ego, says to the 'trapped butterfly': 'no matter how I try to tell your story/ it will, like mine, never be told'. Guff's criticism focuses on insensitive journalists with their headlines – 'There's nothing more forgettable than a headline' – and the one present at a fatal crash who declares: '"That'll make a great story"'. Lawyers too with their legal jargon are called into question. In 'Hobbling' the daughter of a lawyer calls her father 'a liar' and an 'also-ran' yet, as is often the case, the satire lies craftily in the form and pattern of the poem.

Throughout, Guff is a self-confessed, 'exiled clown' wearing the fool's 'cap and bells', daring to be outspoken and to be gifted with smatterings of innate wisdom in the true Shakespearian sense. Movingly, he walks 'the tightrope of the exiled clown' as he knows 'the value of exile/ from others, from himself, from now.' His 'heart is lonely'.

In so many places, Guff accurately mirrors the human predicament. In 'Final Page', he seems stuck in solipsism, trying to recall the forgotten, examining his own humanity as he sits there, like 'a prodigal son' 'as close to home as he is ever/ likely to be'. In the poem, 'Nowhere' he feels totally abstracted from the ordinary life going on around him which he observes objectively, for, sadly, 'Guff is nowhere now,// Nowhere, a place he has long become/accustomed to, both outside and inside'. He is trying 'to be a respected citizen of nowhere', the ultimate definition for an exile, estranged even from himself. Perhaps the only panacea can come in the form of sleep, that 'new country/ where the lost are at home'.

His isolation is worsened by his wariness of human relationships, particularly with women. In 'Recovery' he posits, 'Guess the depth of the river/ between the woman and the man.// If both should venture in/ who will drown?' Some of his caution (and even wisdoms) are embedded in jokey, tossed off lines such as 'He has no wish (he is convinced) to own another./ Possession is a killer of love, the tinker said/ before he became a traveller'. In the poem 'Questions' he goes round in analytical circles regarding possession and ownership, being a loner, a lover and a hater, questions answered only by the woman talking to him: 'Put your questions back in their cage, she said/ and stretch in the freedom of bed'. Questions, ironically, are usually seen as freedom, answers being what is limited and caged.

In 'Nothing says' Guff has the role of adviser and comforter. In his monologue he is addressing someone wronged and bursts into very compassionate speech, demonstrating his true humanity: 'Hurt like yours goes everywhere/ and deepens with each passing year. Guff knows that and that is why/ he listens, looks you in the eye/ and takes, or seems to take a part/ of your deep hurt into his heart,/ lightens your load, increases his own/ and still remains content to listen'. Despite his empathy, Guff is imperfect and acknowledges that he has 'lips the sharpest clamper in town/ his tongue a dark fish behind a rock'. He wants desperately to learn 'how not to hurt', 'when to keep his mouth shut'.

One particularly haunting poem on unrequited love rivals one of Yeats, 'Guff stumped forever', is memorable for its power. Guff is desperate to remember a beloved voice but he cannot. No matter how hard he tries, he finds himself in desert after 'desert of longing'. This 'desert' image is extended into Guff's heartbreaking ache: 'A laughing desert is a merciless thing', 'It turns the sky into mockery of sand'. Isolated in his 'dark cave', 'Darknesses touch each other/ like lovers' awaiting the break-up. He concludes:

Thank heaven for forgetfulness,
Thank heaven for mocking oblivion,
for darkness copulating with darkness,
for Guff stumped forever by a lost voice.

Guff, who often has 'human ingredients of song/ circussing in his head', is aware of the epiphanic power of poetry to uplift.

Guff reads a poem. Yes, words at work
In another country. How come

the same words can rise and fly
like starlings in a September sky

bringing magic to a muddy road.
Words are strange, like the ways of God.

He is capable of breaking out into 'a word-besotted song'. Maybe Kennelly, with Guff, heeds the counsel of the 'dark-faced woman' who urges 'get/ all your songs in order for those not born yet'. If 'those' mean the unborn songs, then let us hope Kennelly will go on to write and write so that, with Guff, we can, as we already surely do, hear his 'words across the years,/ across languages, across the sight/ of starlings enjoying the sky// as if their flying silence will never die'.

Jean O'Brien

The Darning Mushroom

We kept it in an old green sweet tin,
the one we kept the sewing supplies in
the coloured threads, the shiny needles,
buttons, bows, zip, clips, metal fasteners,
even a discarded sewing machine treadle,
a red ladybird pin cushion, anything really.

I asked my mother could I play with it,
use its carved single piece of shaped wood
like a hammer or spin it like a top.
Older I watched my widowed father grapple with it.
Watched as he pulled it through
a sock to mend or the elbow of a jumper.

Saw him thread the tapestry needle
with matching grey or brown wool
and pull it though the eye, then sew
a few parallel lines linking the stretched
fabric, then stitching a crosshatch
until the hole had healed.

Jessamine O'Connor

Silver Spoon

I don't know what to do with the spoon
Found, now, at the back of the drawer
Five old silver spoons bound
Together in an elastic band

But this one, the black one, slid in there
Hidden there
And I know it was me, thinking
I was being clever, that put it there

So it's surfaced now, blackened and filthy
Scorched by history, sudden and smoky
Hideous, but held out in the kitchen light
I nearly don't want to let it out of my sight

You are old times
You are a thousand different moments that were all the same
You are a time capsule with my youth perched inside, grinding
You are magnetism
No one I know now knows what you mean
You are still in my hand
My thumb rubbing your length
And you, the way you feel pressed in my palm.

Following down
My forearm is white, unmarked
Except for the flowers, untracked
Intact, delicate, suddenly precious

The tiny pink petals seem to curl brown
In the curved shadow of the spoon
Still held up to the light of the room
In my deceptively steady right hand

Imagine if the children found it
Behind the sieve, or my mother, visiting
Looking for a corkscrew
I need to get rid of it, before it's too late

We'll march to the lake, just a stroll with the baby
Hurl it out in the air, feel it wrench from my shoulder
And out of my hold, her watching it spin
Silver and black over the water

Fling it so hard I can't splash in
After it, just in case
Because I'm never going to need it again
And if I ever do, any spoon would do

Gill McEvoy

Dusting the Books

On the top shelf dust floats up, thick as bran and chaff:
Tschiffeley's *Ride,* Mary O'Hara's *Thunderhead,*
The Pony Club, the *Spanish Riding School.*

I open a set of *Katy Dids* (prize for English)
and am an awkward child again,
snatching the books from the teacher's hand
in case he might change his mind.

Treasure Island, Kidnapped kept me awake
by torchlight under the sheet.

The deadline sweat of college essays:
midnight panicking through Austen, Bronte,
Dostoevsky, Lawrence, Joyce and Woolf.

Dust down the *Teach Yourself: Italian. Finnish* –
fifty years since I spent summer months in Finland,
freezing lakes, huge moons and silent forests.
Italy I've never visited. But might.

Reacquaint myself with Alison Uttley's
Country Hoard. It told me all the music of the world
lived in the heart of the ash —

what will happen to that music
now the ash are dying?

Tucked among them all, shabby and much read,
the pocket-size *Observer's Book of Wild Flowers,*
a birthday gift when I was eight,

the book that sparked a life-long love of nature.
I open it again and am lost in verges
thick with sanfoin, salad burnet, vetch.

Grace Nichols

Picture My Father

Picture my father, a seriously stylish
Conducting headmaster,
Waving his cane like a wand
Pulling the length of the whole Methodist
Church School into singing –

D'ye ken John Peel with his coat so grey
D'ye ken John Peel at the break of day

Our Demerara voices rising and falling,
Growing more and more golden
Like a canefield's metamorphosis
From shoots into sugar,
The crystal memory shared with a river –

Our Demerara voices moving
To the magic of my father's wand,
Flowing even more sweetly onto
That English maid, deceived by some cad
In a valley below –

O don't you leave me
O don't deceive me

And me, stealing glances through the window
At our own rainwashed, sunbaked landscape
And at my father, working
Under all the accoutrements of empire.
Forty faithful years of being a teacher;

Handing out discipline, harmony, structure –
His gifts, unknown to me then.

Suzanne Cleary

My Father's Feet

My father's feet were
the feet of a Greek statue,
long and narrow, with
a large square toe, but
tender. At the ocean
he hopped across
the sand, wincing
at broken clamshells
and brittle sea grass.
At the lake he ran
across jagged rocks
to plunge with relief
into the icy water.

Of the Aegean Sea
my father would have
said, *It's got nothing
on our Cayuga Lake*.

My father was not
a good swimmer, his kick
a booming fountain
as he laboured.
He did not float,
as did my mother,
with her feathery kick
and the easy glide
he always praised
as he smiled at her
and towelled our hair.

On the day his father died, my father
sat tall in the brown armchair
and cried without covering his face,
his feet heavy on the carpet
in their thick-soled shoes.

To me he was Abraham Lincoln.

There is no record
of Lincoln's feet,
except that he walked
barefoot to school.
In the statues, he always
wears boots, plain,
without strap or buckle.

Like Lincoln, my father
cared nothing for fashion
of any type. For him,
the ancient truths:
Do unto others.
Cast not the first stone.
Unless you are at a lake
and the stone is smooth
and flat and fits, just
so, in your palm.
Then, definitely cast
the first stone.
Show your children how
to cast the second stone,
the third. Then,
agree it is more fun
to collect the stones,
wash them, and carry
them home, where
they will be lost
and then forgotten.

They are just stone.

Louise C. Callaghan

'So like her father'

(an aside, overheard by a small child)

After showing herself off, diaphanous
in a pale organza party frock, she lingers
just inside the door, hidden from view
by the high-backed couch.

The frock, froth-white, standing clear
of her knees. Her washed hair,
white ankle socks and stiff patent shoes –
there she waits for the ripple of their appraisal.

Her grandmother and her mother's sister,
aunt Marie, side by side on the settee.
One or other replies, 'Oh, you mustn't
say that, he doesn't like to hear it'.

Words of lowered conversation:
indelible sunbeams of an afternoon.

Sea Therapy

We're on the beach with Daddy
searching for stones, the right size, the right shape
to skim on water.

I've stopped desiring the tiny coloured ones at last,
the lucid jewels, they're only bits of bottle-glass
run smooth by the tide.

Try and find a good one, it must be flat,
hold it tucked in, yes like that, toward your palm,
curve your pencil-finger, your gun-thumb...

Flung from my grasp, the first one
sits on the water like a lily-pad on the pond
before shimmering down

to the bottom;
another finds the hump of a growing wave
and descends its watery way too.

Us four on the shore bow to the sea's moodiness,
feeding it back its stones. His are more
an offering. Our father

bends level with the flickered surface
and trips his stone like a long sentence over the water
to a faltering three full stops.

Mary Noonan

In the House

I am back in the house, with my father reading
the same paragraph of newsprint, over and over,
as the light fades and the letters break up and slide
over the page and he tries to corral them, dogged
in his conviction that if he keeps herding them,
they will stay there, on the page, in the house where
a trail of tissue-marbles leads to the bathroom, with
its tiny squares of paper, folded over and over, then
laid out in neat rows along the window-ledge. Is it
too late for me to write my prayer on them, open
the window and release the wind horses to the air?

Paper is sacred in this house where every shred
becomes a miniature envelope for elfin letters
posted and collected by the origami master who
spends hours swaying on his wasted hip as day
morphs into night and he sweeps the drift of snow
from the black tiles, or picks each white fleck from
the ribs of his cords. I wish I'd said goodbye
to the man whose step I waited to hear, bounding
up the stairs, whose cool hand I loved to feel
on my forehead, whose 'how's the patient today'
made my heart jump. I wish I'd said goodbye,
before the ancient shape-shifter came to build
his nests of filament, his hillocks of gristle.

Jeremy Page

Abessive

All gone, dutifully recorded
by his linguist father as
the first words he ever uttered,
might equally have been his last.

He'd used himself up by then,
had long since lost his faith
in God, belief in love, his sense
of wonder – inner and outer worlds
now made uniformly monochrome.

His final days saw him return
to his father's beloved case grammar,
discover the abessive. He died
content to have found the word
that summed it all up; though
his last breath is recorded as a sigh.

Note: In case grammar the abessive is used to express the lack or absence of something.

John Griffin

Father of Fire

For My Father

Only the slag drag now and the scrape
of his raking shovel — the metallic din
outside my bedroom window
as coal clangs into a galvanized bucket.

He heaves at the heft and gasps
as though its lift might ease him
back to earth. But no,
there's a dagger's glint
in his flint of blade
that sparks off the concrete,
and now he groans, my minotaur,
he bellows belly-up.

Afterwards, the chimney coughs
his signals out across the gloaming.
Something on wings meets white
and in a flash, in a splash is gone.

Too lazy to rise
he stokes the embers with his eyes,
and as he winks a tear away
the glow vulcanizes of its own accord
into the twilight-conjured grey.

He hugs the last warmth of day.
What retreats back down
the chimney into his lungs
fills the quiet hours.
In the morning his pyre
will be emptied of all
but the perfectly shaped
ash of his fire.

Nigel Prentice

The Dimensions

I raced, hot in the cowboy hat
and six-shooters slapping my thighs
along the whole white face of our house,
cracked path, draggled roses, to surprise
my Dad, to peek around the corner,
catch him napping – but he popped out
from the far end of the wall, gurning
down the long perspective. Doubt
tested again and again, the same
warm shock after I dashed straight back
to the starting corner, or craftily
stole away, turned on my heels: my look
was met by his, two heads at a slant.
Only with time I cracked it: you loped
the length of your wall with adult ease
and covered all my ground. My scope
was my own mad rush, full of myself,
my one perspective. Now I see
behind the scenery, the square faces
and your strides sheer fatherly
application, beating time.
You had more time, and knew more:
now it is mine, while you are still
beyond four walls, and rest there.

Mike Barlow

Back Again to the Town Maze

I come here to find someone, my father, say,
with his bad jokes, familiar arguments,
the brother I wished I had, my wife
before she knew before I did I'd leave her.

This gravel path lost others have trod, privet-
thick walls more than a jump's height high,
sky like a one-track mind. Left, right, left again,
a cul-de-sac and back the way I came

but it never looks the same, like a thought
you try to recall that changes with its thinking,
and always there's a corner unaccounted for,
false memory waiting in ambush.

And here, look, a figure ahead, glancing back
to see if I'm following or check I'm not, gone
by the time I reach the spot to find another
dead-end sending me back on myself,

eyes scanning for clues – dropped ticket,
sweet wrapper, dimp still burning
or freshly bent twig to show this way the trail leads
and there's no knowing where it ends

for the heart with its verdigris sundial
and bent gnomon is no end itself and no centre.
The figure I'm following, who may be following me
could be just yards away, waiting in a cul-de-sac
clutching a ball of string until I've gone.

Lynne Wycherley

Window on the Tide

Finstown, Orkney

We wake to water, a gold dissolve.
A calm sea-current carries the clouds,
small plumes in drifting glaze.

Rain-goose tell me, with your shallow keel,
fulmar with your lime-slung caul,
tight pectorals poised to dive,

can it also carry the freight of the soul,
or like an angel's sandal, the weightless
luminosity of our love?

Magnolia Stellata

Bring me again
to the breathing garden
insects singing
in the scented air
as buds quicken,

lilac and viburnum,
wave cambering
over lit wave
to a taller, white,
intensity –

hints of Kailash
or the Hindu Kush,
a not-quite-snow
or flame –
and I sit

on the rim of heaven.
Life-made-vision.
Hostage to
a hatchery
of stars.

Sally Festing

Figure in a Landscape

I see only the
spill of the February
bright-as-a-bird's-bill
yellow evening sky
and stripped hedges
edging the soon to be
frosted fields, the
hard line of leafless
trees and below them,
a huddle of pines.

Is that you
mother, slipping
from the rawness,
your scarf-wound head
a little on one side,
your white lips
waiting for a kiss?

The wind snaps
like a hound at
the flesh of my face.
You're wearing
a mask and you're
laughing softly, or
is it the shoosh
of the far-off sea
weaving its fingers
into dreams?

And Now Again

Unaware, you've waited for this
for years. To stand on the heart
of the earth lit up by a ray of sun.
Now you're here. Unaware
you've waited for this for years.

The place where the child
you were was at the centre of things,
all her awkward impatience dispersed
by the tides. A place where
the child was at the centre of things.

To stand on the heart of the earth
lit up by a ray of sun. For the child
has grown. And now
you're here – to stand on the heart
of the earth lit up by a ray of sun.

All her awkward impatience
dispersed by the tides. The geese
flying over, cones knocked down
from the pine trees in the wind. All her
awkward impatience dispersed by the tides.

Again you're here. The child
has grown, the geese fly over,
pine trees rock in the wind. The earth
beneath you swells. Once again
you're here at the centre of things.

Faye Joy

A Gower Hotel

Remember the touch of Axminster wool on bare sea-salted feet,
the tiny tiptoe thrills as combed wool curls flatten and reform;
while along that darkened, burnished rail, careering off to swirl
in fashioned arabesques, your fingertips trail in mirrored slips,
and you explore the ineluctable delights of polished wood, and lift
your head to draw in that pervasive smell – *were you really tempted*
to lift heels and haunch to glissade along that rail young girl? –
that palate-teasing warmth snug within the nostrils; you indulge
in the waft of buttery toast, crisp bacon and heat, kitchen heat, more
teasing heat than home could realize. Here, to the muted chimes
of a brass and ebony landing clock, you remember and smile.

The Shape of my Walk

Eyes cast down along the mossy crown
of a nibbled metalled road.
I did not notice him
until that mirage turned
at the crossroad before me.
I hesitated, another figure
from the same direction came
into view, darkly grey, absorbed,
and turned as I intended too.
Our shared and equal spacing
gave a symmetry
to the downhill curve.
Three strangers now evenly ranged,
only a blue bucket, kiltered at the roadside
and a dead fox, mute witness to
this arbitrary shape of my walk.

Will Stone

Departure of the Loved Ones

I watch them both, in their beige raincoats,
obedient, measured, gentle, decent
sucked slowly through passport control
where the traffic is heavy in the heart,
the ungovernable crowds mill, and
the lonely speaker turns dejectedly for home.
My parents in the seats I reserved for them,
my new born elderly children who
navigated the marble steps of Hotel Rubens
and are thoughtful to everyone
because this was their faith, they knew
no religion and were blessed.
Now I watch them recede in a chaos
of technology and systems, of guards
and glass and people who do not know.
I can only imagine the angel
who refused all explanation
guarding them so tenderly
under his great wing.

Robin Renwick

Estuary

Do you have fragments of remembered past
that stand like pinnacles of grass and reeds
above the mudflats, unwashed by the tide,
no idea where they came from
or what they led to – only that they arise,
unsolicited and unrecognised detritus,
from the deepening stream of unconsciousness?

A moment in a foreign bar, a smile,
a stretch of road, the entrance to a wood
where shadows grow, the scent of hyacinths,
echoes of laughter – all I can recall
are broken icons of insignificance,
faceless and timeless – and closing doors
that hide the moments in the enfolding night.

Pearl

I dreamed I was back among the black rocks,
alone with the dead crows and a fear of falling,

woke to sudden rain, and someone calling
your name. My brittle shell has developed cracks

where an old darkness leaks out, and there is sand
in the soft tissue of my complacency.

I hear a door close, trust that you can see
how a dark path is lit up by the laughter of friends.

There was a wind last night, after the rain.
and then stillness, waiting for your return.

Stuart Medland

Island of Shearwaters

It is night.

I sit by the light of a torch
        in the middle of an island with no moon;

There is only wind and rain and ocean
        and the calling of

One hundred thousand Shearwaters –
at sea, once more, themselves, amongst the
thrashing kelp-churned bracken in the

Island dark that
fills the window
at my back. I

Trust them utterly – these sounds
that find me primitive. I
somehow know their
wavering, like the boat that
hardly brought us over.

I go out, once again,
into the tremulous cacophony.

                *

It is the music of hysteria.
A lamentation. Hands, wild
shaken to the heavens in
self-deprecation for
their having to be
Birds at all –
That lay an egg
that needs a nest.

Here's one more –
    in my torchlight, on the rabbit-dropping path –

All shuffle-shrug and, scraping on its keel,
hip-wiggling to be in the burrow,
just as if its legs are tied, its
feet expecting only water,

My illumination in its eyes, my
shine along its graphite,
tube-nose beak.

And so I stand and simply let it happen all around me,
    trying to attune myself, reduce it to its un-disturbing,
        safe, component sounds;

Asthmatic crowing, is it? Or like
squeaky glass – three
fingertips rubbed hard upon the
window's condensation?
One large pebble, maybe,
rolled around a china bowl.

Yet which, regardless of whatever name I put to it,
works every Black-backed Gull
into a frenzy of its own excitement –

Pirates who, by morning,
will have left a hundred Shearwaters
with only their own ocean-soothing,
indigestible, (oh, how ironic)

Wings to fly.

                *

They are outdoing
Oystercatchers, even.
(*'Go to sleep'* they're
piping, *'go to sleep.'*)

And so I try,

But lay awake in bed,
my arms behind my head, like
broken wings themselves –

Imagining I'm at the end point
of the whirling sea, the
birds returning all around my
rain-dark head, about to
batter on the very reef of me, the
draught of salted gale beneath their
wings upon my foolish face –

To keep what vigil I may keep

For every Devil-bird and every
Shipwrecked-mariner's soul.

Note: Skomer Island, a truly other-worldly place which holds the greatest concentration of
breeding Manx Shearwaters in the World (whose story I have only just begun to tell) and
where one may spend a night in their obliging company, courtesy of the South & West Wales
Wildlife Trust.

David Cooke

White-throated Gull

from the Irish of Máirtín Ó Direáin

White-throated gull,
how well it is for you
on the back of the green swell,
its blithe ripples
lapping softly
against your breast.

White-throated gull,
change places today
that I might shake my sadness
riding the sea,
its ripples lapping softly
against my breast.

David Burns

Shoreline

Croft and creel are out of different worlds
but every day there's fish, Susan goes
braced against her basket
to Blackhills, Sunbank, Ardivot, Oakenhead

and waves curl from plough and keel
while the wind rips at their crests
driving dust offshore and spray inland.

Fisher and farmer keep to their own kind
yet Susan once got more than meal or coin
and folk said the burden in front
would balance her load

and sand is at the shore and in the soil
where carts are brought with seaware
to put black heart in the ground.

Susan's loon is dark and thickset.
He married a fisher's daughter
and owns his boat. Men spit and say
he stole to get it

but the tide pushes salt upriver
to mingle with fresh
and pulls it down again, bitter, brackish.

Dusk

We must have gone this round a thousand times
while dogs or the ghosts of dogs got under our feet
before taking off to quarter through the pines.

The broader tracks contain our walking now,
away from the narrow paths, the almost tunnels
that we ran down, chasing, keeping low

for hiding games and later on for loving.
By that fallen tree we had the worst row
and in the copse we had the best forgiving,

what I didn't say then must stay mine.
We're merging into the graininess of dusk
when the path is more remembered than seen.

The sky road, bordered by the trees
will keep us right, if we just look upwards,
trusting the ground and each other. Two crows

slide off a branch and across our minds.
We might just be shapes following someone
who tells how they went this round a thousand times.

Celtic Saints

Fish-lit stream, wood engraving

James Harpur

Columbanus's Journey

My ancient body cried for peace, for death,
As we raised our tents beside the alpine lake.
That night an angel came and shrunk the earth
Before my eyes: one small part glowed, but most
Was pagan dark – what could I do but take
My staff and plod towards the mountain snows?

I wept when we arrived at Bobbio –
I knew it was the end and felt as free
Beside that fish-lit stream as long ago
When leaving home I'd tried to reassure
My flailing mother, who slapped me, hugged my knees
Then rolled across to block the open door

And I had sprung screaming past her body
Knowing that leap would be my longest journey.

Hooded crow, wood engraving

Patrick's Return

I sensed at once the yearning for release.
March mists dispelled the coloured countryside
And hung in curdled webs from ragged trees.

Soft rain soaked fields of stationary bulls
Where gangs of crows were cackling like the druids
Who came to curse me, clacking jaws of skulls.

I sensed the people crying out in sin;
The eyes of severed heads still globed their hell
Of blood and fire, gluttony and drink.

My prayers were sucked from me and overnight
God's love descended like a snowfall.
The blackthorns opened up their petalled light

And everywhere I tapped my staff, my wand,
The fields and trees leapt up to green the land.

Brendan

The naked hermit, cliffs of ice, the cold,
The island of the saints emerging from
Black fog as light, its shore of powdered gold

And apples ripening in every orchard
The youth who welcomed each of us by name –
These died around the settled fires of Clonfert.

But Judas on his rock, wind-burnt, stripped wise,
Writhing above the slaughter of the sea
Remains pristine inside my deepest darkness

His eyes alert for the approach of demons –
I see them glowing as when we rowed away
And hear his voice above the raucous ocean,

'Hell is stasis, keep heading for the sun
And when you reach the light, sail on, sail on.'

Underside of boat, wood engraving

72

St Ita's Lullaby

Hush my sweet Jesus, hush my little lamb
The lamps in Killeedy are flickering to life
Footsteps are failing, the sun's easing down,
Sink into sleep, sleep my little lamb.

Hush my sweet Jesus, hush my little lamb
Streams hug their beds between mossy banks
The straw in the barns is fragrant and warm
Sink into sleep, sleep my little lamb.

Hush my sweet Jesus, hush my little lamb
The wind falls asleep on dark ancient oaks
The moon's dissolving and the night is calm
Sink into sleep, sleep my little lamb.

Hush my sweet Jesus, hush my little lamb
Dream of the angels that drift to the ground
A snowfall of stars until the new dawn.
Sink into sleep, sleep my little lamb.

Hush my sweet Jesus, hush my little lamb
Hush, hush, hush …

Note: James Harpur's poems are part of a forthcoming collaborative work – *A Place Where Ireland is Invisible* – with the wood engraver Pol Ó Colmáin.

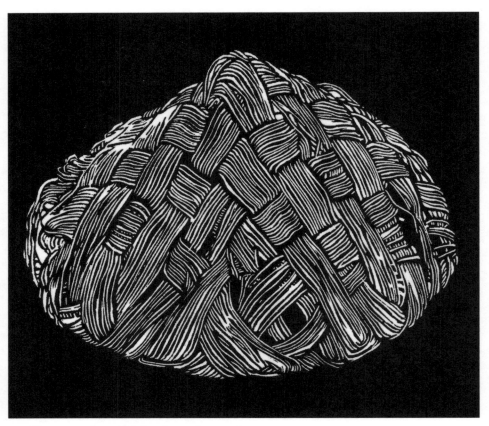

Three strands, or Trí dhual, wood engraving

Ian Enters

Holy Island

i

Particles hold
whinstone rock in place;
prop shale seam
with a shaft beam;
wave-cut lime
from a granite ledge;
layer shape-shift
dunes with marram.

But all is malleable.
Even Pre-Cambrian is
permeable if caught
off-guard by a prayer.

Then particles pulse,
chase the ley lines of Christ
cross-cutting through time
to coalesce with rock
and these flexing dunes.
They ease into mystery,
a cave, where I, Cuthbert,
test the boundaries.

ii

We have waited and waited
for the word to be made flesh
but the estuary remains
an expanse of sand,
causeway a narrow bone.

Suddenly, from the horizon,
a cresting wave, priory high,
launches over the cockle beds
and our waiting is lost
in a cascade of salt
and torrent of prayers.

Vikings invade our island home
and yearning for Messiah is
broken shards from a smashed
tectonic plate. Christ's ley-lines bleed.

The dead will rise. The dead will rise.
We cry, hoisting our burden –
Cuthbert's coffin – on our backs.
Six apostles to carry the load.
Six apostles left to wait.

iii

I, Eadfrith, swear by Aidan's heart
and uncorrupted flesh of Cuthbert
to beautify God's Gospels with
the humility of our Lord
and obstinacy of a donkey.

From the stench of calf-skin,
I strip and bleach vellum.
From brittle lime-stone
I burn white spray.
I besmirch limbs with grime
And score my cheeks with ashes.

Sun finds gold in arsenic,
blue in woad, purple in poison-ivy,
deep red in veins of clagged clay.
Green copper laces the rock shelf
where coracles falter,
and all these glories lie in evil's way
to be transformed by God's word.

I do not know if man,
worshipping idols,
did but play with stuff
to entertain a moment's
hunt upon a wall,
but Lindisfarne words will last
as rock lasts,
as sea lasts,
as love lasts
in the divinity of prayer.

In each generation,
I, Eadfrith, prophesy
others will make dedications
to their maker, as I do now.
My regret is to die before completion.
My consolation lies in knowing
my inadequacies will be forgiven.
For truly I have worked this in God's Name.

Anna Lewis, chosen Broadsheet poet for the second time, was born in 1984. Her poems have appeared in journals including *Agenda, Poetry Wales* and *New Welsh Review,* and her first collection *Other Harbours* was published by Parthian in 2012. She was the chosen young Broadsheet poet in the Welsh issue of *Agenda,* Vol 44 Nos 2-3.

Anna Lewis

Melangell

Its heart was quick against her thigh,
then slowed. She felt the hitching rhythm
of its ribs subside, kept her own breath

as she heard the dogs pant close,
their narrow bodies slit the bracken.
Birds swung up from the slope

and marked the line of their approach;
the saplings shook, then from the trees
poured horses, men in red and gold.

And it was the same as the day
she first stepped onto the sea,
handed herself to the waves

and to the will of God: brash sunlight
thrown back, the green earth
tipping under her feet. Not so much

bravery, not so much faith
as a small, dull light that scratched
into life in her chest, then grew

until she could not see around its edge.
Beyond, there was quiet. The hare
dropped its head to its paws, and slept.

Dwynwen

He was motionless: eyelids snapped back
and lips apart, a silver glaze across his skin.
A fly cleaned its forelegs on his cheek.

She walked once around him,
raised her face to the muscles
that thickened his shoulders,

to his spread fingertips, his palms.
A leaf fell beside him,
a blackbird turned over twigs

at the edge of the path.
On her toes she touched a hand
to his throat. It was cold, and sounded

a smooth, high note; the blackbird
flashed its beak in the dust.
After a while, she bowed her head,

and prayed he might thaw. She stepped
into the trees as water ran out of him,
covered her eyes as he slumped

to the dry leaves and needles,
his legs and arms limp,
mouth loosening into the floor.

Pádraig

This is what the geese saw:
a grey sea and grey Mayo
wrestling the length of the shore,

a white, bulbous moon
buoyed up by the salt,

on the mountain, a man
with arms lifted high and apart.

Deep in the grass: a tremor,
a flinch in the clover,
a flourish of dust on the road.

A pulse passed from the heartlands
out to the coast.

Arms low.
This is all the geese saw.

Gwladys

He used to come home and show me
the blood on his hands, the scraps of hair
stuck to his forearms,

used to hold out to me his stiffened palms
and smile, tired and shining.
Those hands: I took them, raised them, kissed them,

closer to the men he'd spilled
than their own wives, who waited still
for news in muffled, soot-lined huts;

between women, my salute.
All that is gone, since our son
held out his faith, his face above it lit;

now each night, between the leafless trees
we wash: the water slices off
our shames, our cruelties.

I watch my husband's silver chest,
his silver stomach cut up from the lake,
armfuls of water hours from ice

thrown back and forth across the breadth of him.
He comes to me wreathed in steam;
his breath condenses on my cheek.

Note: Anna Lewis's poems re-imagine moments from the lives, or stories, of four fifth- and sixth-century saints. Melangell, who fled from Ireland to Powys to escape an unwanted marriage, shelters a hare from hunters. Dwynwen, in the forests near Brecon, prays for the restoration of her suitor, who after he attacked and raped her was turned into ice. Pádraig or Patrick, who travelled from Britain to Ireland as a slave and again later as a missionary, banishes all snakes from Ireland. Gwladys and her husband Gwynllyw, two warriors in Glamorgan, abandon their violent way of life after their son Cadog converts to Christianity.

Ben Smith, chosen Broadsheet poet, 29, is a writer and occasional lecturer based in the South-West. His poetry, fiction and criticism have appeared in various magazines, journals and anthologies. He is an editor of *The Clearing*, an online magazine promoting writing about place. His first pamphlet of poetry will be published by Worple Press in Autumn 2014. He is currently working on a collection of poetry about wolves.

St Ronan's Chapel

The stones give no answers.
The cracks in the mortar admit only threads of sky.
Stone bench,
stone altar;
if there were books they would be bound in stone.

No sound finds its way down the long, low tunnel
to shelter from the wind –
not the storm petrel's lost-soul laughter,
not the seal's soft wailing
stretching over the surrounding waters.

All we know is that *Ronan* means *little seal,*
as though one of those creatures,
wondering at the new shapes crossing
the straits, the lights on distant cliffs,
rose one day and walked inland,

shedding blubber and fur in the milk-white shallows,
taking a new skin of rough cloth
washed ashore in a storm.
And perhaps this darkness and silence
is not the result of a man's search for wilderness,

but an attempt by something wild
to turn its back on the light of the sky
and the clamour of the waves,
to see its world through our eyes,
hear it through our ears.

The Stone Boats of the Saints

We need no wind for our stone boats,
we don't need to wait for the tide.
We need no canvas, no pitch, no rope
no benches, no ballast, no oars.
We need no tools for our stone boats,
they are already there, by the sandless shore –
black granite hulls among the limestone's grey angles
like weights and measures
left over from the workings of the world.

We are searching for beginnings –
thumb-prints on the cliffs,
the first sketches of islands beyond the rim of the sea.
We have no charts to find our way.
We need no moon, no stars,
just our stone boats seeking out fellow stone.
We haul them into the slate-grey waters.
Our path lies ahead of us, bright as a seam of quartz.

The Keeper of the Sands

At dawn, unseen, he walks out
across the vast moon-surface of the bay
to find the safe paths, to gauge
how far the sand stretches today
before it turns restless –
all depth and movement and weight.

A bad way to go – sucked under
by the distant pull of a flat grey sea.

He's seen horses dragged under,
carts loaded with cockles and shrimp,

and once he fell waist deep into the grip of it
– no birds, no wind, just the sand and its silences –

waited hours for enough firmness to return
to lever himself free.
Like breaking open a dead man's fist
finger by finger.

Even now, walking out, he feels it –
the tug, the final heavy slump of himself gone under.
Eyes heaped with sand, mouth brimful with sand.
The endless wash of sand and water.
The restlessness. The endless turning.

He puts down one foot and then the other.
This far out, there are no hard edges,
nothing fixed,
just his last pegged-out paths
where things hold for a time,
just the places where his footprints appear
or disappear
as he makes and unmakes the borders
of his world of shifting sand and water.

Peregrini

I set myself adrift
               in a coracle upon the sea
circling on tides
          and prayers
and tar-soaked skin.

I was lashed to the oars, braced
against the wicker-work,
               feeling the wave tips
for the channels to the grey edge of the world.

The islands appeared through the spray
like cataracts in my salt-scorched eyes.

I have known such depths of water
and such depths of sky –

each day the waves beat through the sea stacks
and clouds piled up to the stars.

I learned to measure the time by the moon
and the months when laver and kelp
were thrown up onto the cliffs.
But there was another, slower time

of rainwater filling a row of clay pots

and strips of fish drying and curling on the stones.

At night I lay under the shell of my coracle,
listening to the rush of gulls
returning to land   the wing-beats
in my blood

and I set myself adrift
circling
         through the sky's fathoms.

River Burial

Water grips me tighter than soil.
They levered me from the graveyard clay,
bound me, hauled me,
sank me in the river's pale sand.
They befuddled me.
Every time I try to gather my thoughts
they scatter into pools
                              of light and shade
where tadpoles struggle
in their jellied sacks
and just-hatched damsel-flies
                                    pry themselves
from a surface tough as cat-gut.

Trout swim themselves to stillness
waiting for a slack in the flow.
But I must wait longer,
until the leaves begin to fall
and I can sift through to find
my one small thought,
until the night
                    when all the edges turn
thin and grey
and I can drag myself up
                              – waist-deep,
knee-deep –
among the charcoal stubs of the trees
and try another faltering step
towards home.

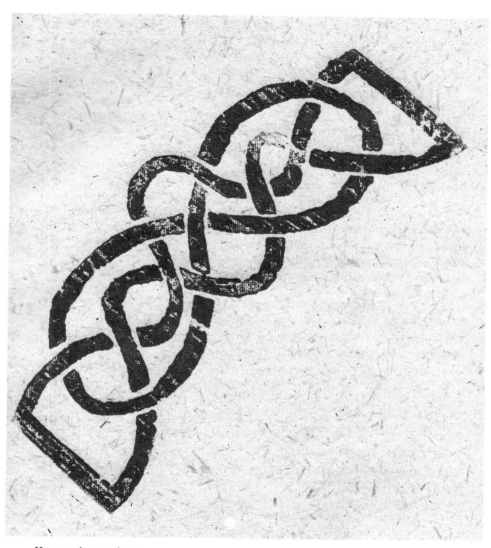

Knotwork, wood-cut

Kiran Millwood Hargrave,

Chosen Broadsheet poet, 23, is currently studying at Oxford University. She is the author of a pamphlet, *Scavengers* (British Shakespeare Association, 2011), and two collections, *Last March* (Pindrop Press, 2012) and *wide-shining* (79 rat press, 2013). Her work has appeared in many journals and anthologies, including the *Sentinel Annual Literary Anthology 2012*. Gatehouse Press published her third collection *Estuary* in October 2013.

Selkie

On the emptied beach I turn from the waves
from the smooth tug of the Yesnaby tide
towards you, backed by limestone caves,
then unstitch myself at the hip and step out.

I have come for you. Open your hands to me
in the rain, in the dark cloister of Skaill bay.
Listen: how the sea shrugs itself up the beach
struggles to cast itself off, like a shadow at midday.

After, I grope for my seal pelt in the darkness.
It is quiet now, the sea far out and closed,
a riddle I forgot I was meant to know.
A tithe of scum wrinkles my toes.

You sing me lullabies, wrap me in your history
until it feels almost-shared. You kiss me
until you're dizzy with sea-breath, and fling
your laugh out to the heaving black.

A whole night passes, then is gone.
The day drags the water back up to us
and I drape myself into form.
At the tide line I pause, turn again to you.

Let me
drop my skin. I never liked the sea.
Let me
lie down with you again.
Let me
stay. I could love you.

Pebble

It sat beside them on the dinner table
pressing down a page as he read aloud

to her, against the wind
from the Minack,

dropping notes like stones
through the open window,

and later stretched the red distance
between his palm and her nape,

called down a week of rain,
some darkness, a stitch of time.

The night sinks into its element –
a simple grace of silence –

as the pebble on the mantel
unhatches the sea.

Persephone

Most mornings I can barely stand to look at this
something-like-happiness misting our periphery,
an epiphany spat out like pips from our tongues,
all our half-sung songs stringing along behind us,
and you, dark god, perfect weight above me, telling me
you love me and me drop dropping droplets through your hand
my stolid body turning liquid as sand and running our fierce current
fast as silver-quick fish, my flick-flecking lips biting like teeth
as I shoal beneath you, held so tight I can barely breathe.

The shift of the seasons sinks us,
and at my brink I tip through
summer autumn winter spring
– all the fast-spin of cold and heat –
fells me as I fall back replete,
my heart beating pomegranate red,
jawing my mouthful of seeds.

Web

It is a peculiar cold that they arrive in,
The suitors. Like marbles
They roll into the crevices of our stalled home,
Bounce off the walls with drink.
Feasts and contests keep them at bay
While I watch the low curve of the sea from my window
In my widow's weeds, spider-black,
Waiting for the sail-break in the horizon
That means you are home.
At further insistence
I distract them with dancers from the north,
Their hips coiling like smoke.
This holds them for a month at least,
But then it is time to go for broke.
I begin a wedding dress
On my spinning wheel strung with silk.
I order dyes from Galilee, that open place
Of pearls and coral and space.
When it is finished, I will wed one of them,
These un-fine men.
I work the thread, feeding it fast
And the bodice blooms beneath my fingers.
The suitors are pleased.
They drink themselves dreamless
And that night I sneak to the spinning-room,
Pluck out a string at the heart of the dress,
Unspool it from the chest.
I will continue to unpick these threads that bind
Until I have lost sight of you,
Or until I have lost my mind.

Up

'She's dead as earth'.
King Lear

Beneath the sandstone conduits and veins of quartz
that stripe my side like impossibilities
and lower still to the earth's end and the beginning of the unknown
lies my base. Solid, heat, imagined black and cuppable in a palm,
rubbed smooth like obsidian. Then iron courses writhing, drawn round
like a clock face – there is no stepping through but if you do –
my mantle, de-furred and unyielding – break this
and I come open with words words words:
igneous basalt granitic amphiboles schists granulites
like great cysts waiting to be spurred.
Nose your way up further still and find the sea in me,
marinas crystallised into sandstone, shale,
Auden's rock, his praise still audible
and ringing round
the frozen bubbles
caught hard and still –
a silence here,
many moments
stopped.

Push further and clasp the soil,
shifting through tree roots,
sifted by grasses and earthworms
a thin wrapper layering me in;
and perched on top,
two fools shouting at the wind.

Patricia McCarthy

Choir Singers: Don Paterson and John Burnside

Don Paterson: *Selected Poems* (Faber, 2012)
John Burnside: *All One Breath* (Jonathan Cape, 2014)

Don Paterson's *Selected Poem* is a testament to the ongoing achievement of a gifted, interesting, timeless voice in UK poetry today. Cullings from his four volumes show him to be a virtuoso of the profound, the amusing, the ironic, the passionate and the earthy, even of the surreal and the macabre.

Notes on Paterson's highly accomplished versions of Rilke's *Orpheus* were featured in the double Rilke issue of *Agenda, A Reconsideration of Rainer Maria Rilke* vol 42 Nos 3-4, and, in an earlier issue of *Agenda, An Anthology of New Poetry* Vol 37 No 4 (while founding editor William Cookson was still alive), his moving versions of Machado's *The Eyes* were reviewed by me. It is interesting to note that in his *Selected Poems*, chosen by the poet himself, he includes two substantial sections from both books.

Here is a man not afraid to orchestrate his voice in all its ranges, a man who increasingly, throughout this volume, is seen to develop his craft to great effect; a musician who, in accordance surely with his Scottish roots, appears at heart to be a consummate balladist. Unlike many dry, clever but impersonal male poets writing today, he dares use his life experience to make his poems ring with authenticity. The 'I' (whether a personal or poetic one) is not vetoed, probably the influence of Machado who wished his voice to be direct and uncluttered: 'It's not the true/ I the poet's after,/ it's the you'. Also, like Machado, in Paterson's later work especially, it seems that he has obeyed Machado's instruction: 'Light your poem from two angles/ one for the straight reading,/ one for the sidelong'. It is with this very 'sidelong' angle, that Paterson weaves his erudition, and challenges the reader.

Like many other poets/version-makers/translators (Martyn Crucefix, Harry Guest, Michael Hamburger, Will Stone come to mind), it is interesting to ask the question whether there is a dichotomy between the 'translated' works and the poet's own poems. Indeed, in this *Selected*, it does seem that Paterson has been positively influenced by both mentors, distilling their work so discretely into himself, that they speak out in strands of his voice, adding vision and depth. He himself said in his articulate and analytical 'Appendix : Fourteen Notes on the Version' to his *Orpheus: A Version of Rainer Maria Rilke* (Faber): 'Versioning allows a poet to disown their own voice and try on another. This voice might fit well, or might fit badly. When the poet returns to reclaim their old voice, it either no longer quite fits, or has altered, having apparently kept some strange company of its own in the meantime. Sometimes it has just disappeared. None of this is ever regretted'.

It is pertinent, in this light, to focus on the poems written after *The Eyes* and *Orpheus*. Of course there are early gems such as 'Sisters' in which he fancies the twin of his lover. His lover is intimately described in startlingly original imagery: 'As the sun spread on her freckled back/ I felt as if I'd turned the corner/ to a bright street, scattered with coins;/ for weeks I counted them over and over'. Another beautifully accomplished early love poem is 'The Trans-Siberian Express': 'I follow your continuous arrival' and the lovers share 'a lifetime of days'. The long, ambitious poem, 'Nil Nil', is clever, full of life and with amusing details such as 'big tartan flasks/ open hatchbacks parked squint behind goal-nets,/ the half-time satsuma', the 'grim fathers and perverts with old English Sheepdogs', 'wee Horace Madden/ so smelly the air seems to quiver above him'. The scene then switches somewhat surreally to a small aircraft crash, the pilot killed: 'the tank blew/ and made nothing of him, save for his fillings./ his tackets, his lucky half crown and his gallstone'. Finally the poet himself appears in the poem, addressing the reader, *'the plot thinning down to a point so refined/ not even the angels could dance on it. Goodbye'*. In this early poem we see the poet already touching on the numinous, a little akin to Seamus Heaney in his football poem 'Markings', a fairly late poem, on whose homemade pitch at dusk, the boys 'were playing in their heads'. In the strong poem, 'A Private Bottling' on the theme of unrequited love, Paterson makes 'an ancient pledge of passionate indifference', 'wishing her health as I might wish her weather'. Yet the landscape has broadened out;

> I carefully arrange a chain of nips
> in a big fairy ring, in each square glass
> the tincture of a failed geography,
> its dwindled burns and woodlands, whin-fires, heather,
> the sklent of its wind and its salty rain,
> the love-worn habits of its working folk,
> the waveform of their speech, and by extension
> how they sing, make love, take a joke.

There is the lover, in the poem 'The Lover', 'who fills/ your name full of her breath again'; there is the repeated line 'No one slips into the same woman twice' from the sexually explicit poem, 'from Advice to Young Husbands'; the finely achieved, 'Candlebird' with its refrain:

So take my hand and tell me, flesh or tallow
Which man I am tonight I leave to you.

And so on. Highlights, for me, after *The Eyes*, in which there is a definite
progression towards universals, are 'Luing' which is beautifully handled on
two levels in that 'sidelong' way. The place to go to after 'emptiness' is

> our unsung
> innermost isle: Kilda's antithesis,
> yet still with its own tiny stubborn anthem,
> its yellow milkwort and its stunted kye.

There, the persona will be 'deeper/ in her arms than ever – sharing her breath'.
In 'such intimate exile' 'the first touch of light will finish you'. 'St Brides:
Sea-Mail' is a really 'big' poem, honed and handled to perfection about an
oil slick damaging, even killing, many birds.'The Forest of the Suicides',
after Dante, is powerful, rhythmical and full of narrative expertise as is 'The
Hunt'. Paterson's learning is always subtly in service of the poetry.

'Letter to the Twins', headed by a quote from Plutarch, is full of advice to
sons about 'the honouring of your lover' and how to make love. Paterson's
language is explicit but lyrical which makes for delicacy:

> Then, as you break, at once you understand
> how the roses of her breast will draw in tight
> at your touch, how that parched scrubland
> between her thighs breaks open into wet.

'The Wreck', written in rhyming couplets, is an extraordinary tour de force
as a love poem, starting straight off with the exclamatory:

> But what lovers we were, what lovers,
> even when it was all over –

The passion is at its height and drunken and the pair 'mine' their 'lovely
secret wreck'.

His 'White Lie', and the later 'The Lie' poems are very humorous, and
tongue in cheek. A couple of poems are more directly reminiscent of Carol Ann
Duffy, such as 'The Reading' which is satirical, witty, with classical allusions,
conversational tone, short, punchy phrases like 'Bloody kids', and the subtext
which probably says more than the surface text with its implications.

The poems chosen from *Rain*, the last section in the book, after the Rilke, are on the whole quieter, almost primitive with their nursery-rhyme sound; in this case the going backwards represents paradoxically a progression. Their deceptive simplicity is Blakean, many being addressed tenderly to children, born and unborn, including his own. It is as if, like Rilke, Paterson is humbly and genuinely trying, now, to 'say the unsayable'. In 'The Day', for example, he states: 'We are not chosen, just too far apart/ to know ourselves the commonplace we are'. He stresses the angst of the existentialist. Despite the woman protagonist saying to her man, '"Well, it's a miracle I found you/ in all this space and dust"', Paterson underlines the isolation of the individual: '"Think: all of us/ as cut off as the living from the dead"', each person being, as John Donne concurred, 'a separate universe'. The solipsism of the individual is highlighted:

> We talk, make love, we sleep in the same bed –
> but no matter what you do, you can't be me.

In the penultimate elegiac short sequence, 'Phantom', addressed to the poet's friend, Michael Donaghy who died very suddenly and unexpectedly at the height of his poetic powers, the latter becomes a third mentor for Paterson. In the first poem, the night has a sinister power of its own. While Donaghy spoke, it was 'switching off the mirrors in their frames/ and undeveloping your photographs'; it then 'slipped into a thousand murmuring books/ and laid a black leaf next to every white'. Parts II, III and IV are ekphrastic poems, focusing on the Spanish sixteenth century artist, Zurbarán and his 'Saint Francis in Meditation'. Like Yorick, Saint Francis is holding a skull which movingly links to the very end line of the sequence: 'I put down Michael's skull and held my own'. The poet's 'I' becomes 'we': 'we arrest the saint mid-speech' similar to the way Donaghy must have been arrested mid-speech in his sudden death. V and VI and VII are memorably powerful meditations demonstrating Paterson's growth in stature, and rounding off the sequence with their tour de force as Paterson tries to come to terms with the void, with becoming 'nothing', yet with a possible transcendence of death for the universal human spirit. 'We are ourselves the void in contemplation./ We are its only nerve and hand and eye'. Yet 'when the mind rests and the dark light stills', 'the open book/ (will) turn runic and unreadable again./ and if a word then rises to our lips/ we speak it on behalf of everything' Donaghy's voice and life with its 'drunken hopscotch' comes through with realistic slang and spirit: '*I loved the living but I hated life*'. Donaghy does not want to be canonised by death, nor for his poetry to be valued beyond the talent he humbly insists he had. In terms of the great meditative philosophers, there is the hint, in Donaghy's rhetorical question, that even all art becomes nothing:

what kind of twisted ape ends up believing
the rushlight of his little human art
truer than the great sun on his back?

Paterson's conclusion of the poem, 'The Landing' demonstrates his appreciation of being gifted with bardic powers:

No singer of the day or night
is lucky as I am
the dark my sounding-board
the light my auditorium.

As his poems flicker between dark and light, we, the readers, are honoured with his song.

*

John Burnside's voice is one and the same throughout his collections, always recognisable. His lines flow naturally with such apparent ease that his poems are so like breath – Fiona Sampson calls his work 'rapt, floating verse' – that the reader is inclined to think: I wish I had written that.

Not so easy, though, really, to acquire this special fluency, as if Burnside is simply speaking the lines out without having to compose them. Unlike Paterson, who seems to be growing into the numinous, Burnside remains consistently in touch with the other side of things, with what constitutes our mortality here on earth, and in this way he resembles Rilke.

This arresting new collection flows into all Burnside's previous collections, attesting to the significance of the whole oeuvre. Here are man's eternal questions: is 'happiness' possible here on earth, and perhaps a 'quiet' the best that can realistically be achieved; who is the true 'self' and should this self, through analysis and depersonalisation, become a no self; is imperfect man destined always to live unfulfilled, dwelling secretly on what could/should have been? What constitutes a real 'home' continues to be a dominant theme. In the interview between Burnside and myself in the *Dwelling Places* issue of *Agenda: An appreciation of John Burnside* Vol 45 No 4/Vol 46 No 1, having admitted that when he first read Dao De Ching, he felt at home (though it wasn't a case of falling in love with 'Eastern Mysticism'), he says, 'I'd rather follow the path of homelessness to wild dwelling than accept the costly shelter of a certain kind of building – building that displaces, violates and domesticates what some have called, in translation and as a kind of shorthand, *the great spirit*. And 'home, like grace, is a temporary, sometimes fleeting thing, and cannot be occupied as such'.

In *All One Breath*, then, home can be a place never found when, on his grandmother's death, the boy he was 'kept walking into blizzard, dumb to grief,/ and nothing he could track to bring him home'; it can be a place longed for but not found 'through love and loss of love/ to this finale, orphaned, far from home'; it can be the deceptive 'tallowed gold of home, ringed round with vines,/ a single lantern/ in the attic window'; it can be a real worked-for place such as his grandmother had and became 'proud' to call the place her own

> by making a garden of sorts from the pit town's
> clinker and soot, her flowerbeds
> thick with bees,

Yet even she, like the poet, loved most 'variegation/ hairstreak, the broken line, the not quite/ finished of the moments'... 'Nothing defined, the world/ all guesswork: birds,/ then shadows'. After her death, the poet envisages her new home in the after-life as somewhere he 'can't make out'.

So it can be anywhere – his little sister found, when she went missing, she was 'suddenly at home,/ no matter where she was'. 'Home', perhaps at its best, can be more intangible 'as love and narrative', 'the house shrugged off'. As he said in the interview 'Home is there until we try to pin it down'. In 'VII Self Portrait as Picture Window' he talks of

> some lost art
> of finding home in sheep trails, lines of flight,
> the feel of distance singing in the flesh
> and happiness-as-forage, bedding in,
> declining, making sense of what it finds.

The seeming resignation to the imperfect in life and the unachieved that prevails in many of the poems is relieved by a special 'quiet like the ceasing of a drum' which allows for glimpses of epiphany and the feeling of safety – 'happiness being the knowledge/ that someone is safe'. And it is this 'quiet', this 'safety' and moments of epiphany such as 'a wave of longing in the blood-lit dark// for what we are/ beyond the things we seem', or 'the flicker of sky in our bones/ that is almost flight' that constitute this 'happiness', or the 'makings of bliss' we can see in lyrical images if we look back.

Like Paterson, Burnside brings in touches of the macabre, and illuminates, as well as light and its colours, a dark side. For example, even his grandmother's epiphany is tinged with decay as she recalls 'a last frost burning away/ the night-time shapes of twisted/ plum trees/ and the empty branches strung/ with skin and stones/ like tender nubs/ of canker'. Burnside has spoken of accepting, like the animists, 'the cycles of life and death that individuate us', and of the 'dark celebration' that this involves – 'one in which the tragic has its place, but a celebration nonetheless'.

He also admits to 'the savage, interior self, the dark enemy, the wild and wilderness, all that seems resistant to the growth of the known and the corporate village'. For example, in what seems to be a love poem, 'All You Need', the persona feels love at a remove, 'like the story he has longed/ for years to tell'; however, as soon as he mouths the words *'love you'* to the girl, he is filled with a kind of horror and it seems that it was just 'for show' – the 'line that runs so far from what he meant/ it frightens him that thinking made it so'. In 'The Couple', the male is bored with his partner and begs her 'for pity's sake' to fantasise like himself and to pretend that she is 'alone/ as I have done for years, in borrowed rooms// with other bodies/ waking with a start/ to sweat and hair, a cling of heat and skin/ I barely know'. This seems the only way to keep the relationship fresh and physical, perhaps pessimistically, but then there is a double twist as he will then be able to remember her 'as once I thought you, when I thought you true'. Here, as elsewhere with 'secrets', the poet is taking the 'sidelong' angle as Paterson frequently does, making us question his partner.

The personal self, the ego, the 'I', the one with the child always in him, is one to lose in life's strange 'theatre': 'whatever happens in the life to come/ you'd hardly want to drag the self along'. This 'self', along with the 'slender, puppet versions' of himself, is often depersonalised until 'it isn't me at all', or is pluralised, for example, in the 'pause for the briefest/ rehearsal of someone else/ at the back of my mind,// the soul friend' of whoever the persona is – who has 'come to the end' of his 'picture book world'. These examples are backed up by Burnside's own words: 'It's not my inclination to lack a self; I just don't want to have a fixed self, something to get attached to. I want to live – and die – as fully as I can and "self" could well get in the way of that'.

This collection has an unusual focus: through mirrors, fog, through 'breath-fogged windows', attesting to what he has called his 'fuzzy thinking' which illustrates 'how everything is in flux'. Their reflections, often distorted, provoke revelations. Film, too, is a recurring image, with its 'grainy footage' and names of film stars thrown in. He tells us in the *Agenda* interview: 'a reel of film, maybe the first film ever made that still exists but is now so old that almost nothing appears when it's projected, nothing but enticing shadows and flickers... That's where I like to dwell – in that old film. It's always running somewhere in my mind'. Other poems deliver up their images and truths through self portraits, still lives, lithographs, lithogravure and paintings. Elegies, resurrections (e.g. of his father), ecological concerns, keenly observed nature and animal poems as detailed and accurate as any of Ted Hughes' are part of the varied mix.

The 'knotwork of the heart' is a recurring motif. He, or the persona, refutes the later Yeats' 'foul rag and bone shop of the heart': 'I've never thought the heart was rag and bone/ only a looking glass'. When he examines this organ, 'each heart becomes/ a species in itself, the sound it makes/ /distinctive, one more descant in the dark./ before it disappears into the marshes'. Both the 'looking glass' image and the 'disappearing' show the heart reduced, losing its beat perhaps. Yet he honours the heart in 'Earth', summoning

> redwoods veined with centuries of light
> and the faint but indelible stain of a living man
>
> who died because he trusted to the earth
> the heart he had kept intact, though no one in these parts
>
> speaks any longer of heart, or the sound in the trees
> that once was a spirit and now is no more than the wind.

Here in his 'sidelong' way, with a hint maybe of Christ, he points to what is lost in the world today.

Pervading the collection is the sense that we are all sharing the same lot here on earth for the duration of our brief life-spans, and even in our after-lives when we might return to co-exist with the living as ghosts, 'disputing the imposition of linear time'. Parallel with this, Burnside feels strongly that 'poetry is a heightened way of saying *Look how thoroughly we are all in this together*', 'the weather of a heart/ so commonplace, you think it must belong//to someone else'.

In this haunting collection, Burnside definitely conceives life (to quote from 'Alcools') 'as a hymn tune'. He manages (see the last line of 'Instructions for a Sky Burial') 'new breath and vision, gathered from the quiet'. The first poem in the collection, ending with 'everything/ is choir', beautifully links in a bookend pattern to the last poem's grand finale:

> like as not, most everything runs on
> as choir: all one; the living and the dead:
> first catch, then canon; fugal; *all one breath*

wedding it to the title.

W S Milne

Public Men: Rowan Williams and Grey Gowrie

Rowan Williams: *The Poems of Rowan Williams* (Carcanet Press, 2014)
Grey Gowrie: *The Italian Visitor (*Carcanet Press, 2013)

Rowan Williams' book is a straight reprint of the Perpetua Press (Oxford) edition of 2003, and is a sign of a public keen to read the former Archbishop of Canterbury's poetry. Rowan Williams is a very fine and important writer in the line of Christian contemplatives. In his poetry (and to a lesser extent, I would argue, in his prose) he brings a fierce intellect to bear on the complexities and glories of the Christian passion. His work lies within the long Anglican tradition of John Donne, George Herbert, Thomas Traherne, Henry Vaughan, and R S Thomas. Dr Williams is very much aware of the depth of this tradition, and his reliance upon it. In his book on Dostoevsky he writes 'We are bound to use words that have histories and associations'. The primary fact of history for him is the life and death of Jesus Christ, and the living fact of faith upheld in a culture which largely tries to ignore it:

> Whistling across the centuries of blood
> on the grass, and the hard light of pain ...
> Don't you know?
> says the whistling, Don't you remember?

Faith for Williams is a fact which binds us to community, a value he believes is endangered by our current 'civilisation'. He writes of 'what human beings owe to each other' in an age he argues in which 'the disappearance of religious belief' is not so much 'a triumph of reason but the harbinger of reason's collapse'.

Now, this may sound all very good in theory and may position a writer securely on the pulpit of homiletics, but the impressive achievement of Williams' work is that he succeeds in carrying his convictions over into poetic practice, into imaginative fact. Eschewing solipsism (what he terms 'the frustrated self') as alien to belief, but importantly not ignoring the difficulties and bitterness of 'the mind's sour spit', he creates what he calls (in his essay on R. S. Thomas) 'a poetry of honest religious utterance' which is also at the same time 'an articulation of uneasy faith':

Lands before commerce, loss, desire
Voice on the thorn complaints and bargaining;
Before the showers come back to dig the moor
With metal hollows mined down to the vein.
A, says the wind, and when the first rain falls,
O, says the scarred pool round its fractured spines.

This brings the freshness of Christian faith to bear on the writing of lyric
verse, a quality which we have not heard in English poetry for some time,
I would argue. This faith is not in any way complacent (the tone of its
expression is in fact often hesitant), but is grasped as difficult, and as an
honest struggle with 'self-deception', all the entangled, nightmarish 'tendrils
of human fantasy and self-deceit' – anger, shame, impenitence, guilt – which
limits the potentiality of selfhood:

Here is the world entire. And in the middle
of all the words, who is hiding? ... the sound of the deep
is an abyss of silence...
World given for world...

This is what he calls (again in his essay on Thomas) 'the experience of living
over dark fathoms', 'the Kierkegaardian void over which faith balances', 'the
immeasurable distance of God's being in the depth of the prosaic human life
of Jesus'. Faith here, in the context of Williams' poetry, coalesces with his
firm conviction that imagination is the spring-head, or well, of the human
spirit, and cannot be held within the confining forms of doctrinaire belief only.

In the clear winter pastures of the stars
is innocence, a soft and stinging dark...
infancy, a soul unhistoried...
the fields of sheep, the fresh and unimagined
scents of spilled grass or leaf...
The dripping dawn around
Confirms the unformed fear. The world can change...

The imagination, then, possesses this transforming power of the spirit.
That 'change' is the darkening 'knowing mortal child', experiencing 'the
spiky consonants of Canaan', all that which is treacherously articulate
and reasonable, a vision of 'choked foundations' and 'ancient agony', not
unlike Blake's *Songs of Innocence and Experience*. But perhaps 'Jerusalem'
provides a better analogy:

And thine the Human Face, and thine
The Human Hands and Feet and Breath,
Entering thro' the Gates of Birth
And passing thro' the Gates of Death.

Williams' poetry similarly endorses the dialogue between 'the incarnate spirit' and 'the unadorned absolute' (the phrases come from his book on Dostoevsky) in terms of 'the baking dust' of death, a vision of the earth after the unregenerate 'clay-daubed hands' of man first shaped their way 'in the noisy air of the world':

He will come, will come,
will come like crying in the night,
like blood, like breaking,
as the earth writhes to toss him free.
He will come like child.

So it is in these poems, salvation is seen to lie (not over-dogmatically, however) with those who are 'ready to receive/ Christ laid on them like a cloth', so that Williams' faith (not inerrable, but human) is seen as 'grounded in a recognition and affirmation by nothing less than God'. He says: 'I watch the silent sky without doubt…/I reach out breathless to the shore.' Faith is 'the clean stone from which we can refashion our image', restoring it, 'rinsed at last/to its sharp grain' again, cleansing 'diseased perceptions of reality', and 'the great Lord realised'. This poetic vision arises from a critical belief that 'the material world apprehends, transmits and embodies eternal reality'.

Poetry, for Rowan Williams, is imagination working at the highest pitch of language and attention. In his prose he argues that poetry 'realises the given in a new way… pushing the inner tensions of language to the point of new discoveries in form and metaphor'. Even more definitively, he argues (I think incontestably) that 'poetic apprehension is essential to being a human self', and that such a force opposes the ubiquity of all that is 'mechanical, functional, impatient', all that separates us, as he sees it, from God. Not that this is an easy, facile step to take. Far from it. 'God', he says, 'has to be rediscovered in every age', and requires bravery (see especially his poem 'After Silent Centuries: For the Catholic Martyrs of Wales'). He argues, for instance, that 'the Dostoevskian novel… is an exercise in resisting the demonic and rescuing language', an attempt to evince an image or symbol (sometimes he says 'icon') of what a 'morally coherent life' might look like, pitting itself against 'a culture of banality and self-interest', demonstrating 'a constant and unfinished interplay of perspectives', that press home 'the light provided by faith', whilst acknowledging 'the challenges of failure, suffering, and desolation' in a Pascalian dispensation.

Once understood, such a position can provide a glimpse of a coherent future countering contemporary cynicism, one which can repel our putative 'moral and imaginative destitution'. In this creative way, Williams can concentrate on the figure of the true martyr (as opposed to what he calls the false, 'the murderously spiritual' kind) as an exemplar of pain and suffering, foregrounding the reality of sacrifice and its ethical implications. The position is realised in the body of Williams' own work:

> Grace, yes, but damnation too dissolves
> in place ... eluding the imagination ...
> The wounds as fresh as ever ...
> Iron and bitter, bright like life ...

What holds Rowan Williams' considerable poetic imagination is not our fortuitous, accidental self ('a process, fluid and elusive' as he terms it) but the self (or soul, if you like) in its 'eternal worth':

> How long before the flesh has split the bark?
> ... The dust-choked distance? While we wait to see
> A waking earth that stirs into the sun...

Miracle is as evident here to the poet as necessity is to the practical man (the public figure of authority), a deep articulation of belief:

> And I, while there is breath left to me,
> Say, Thanksgiving, with a hundred thousand words.
> Thanksgiving: that there is a God to worship...

His poetry, then, is not autonomous; its roots lie in his faith, in 'the particular human agony in front of us', and in the 'afterthought of gift':

> It will be
> Oh, such a daybreak, such bright morning,
> When I shall wake to see him
> As he is.

Rowan Williams' poetry is often as tender as George Herbert's, and relies for its power on the same faith. There is no doubt that he is a significant religious poet.

Grey Gowrie's *The Italian Visitor* is an impressive sequel to *Third Day: New and Selected Poems*. What strikes one on first reading Gowrie is just how different his voice is from the rest of the contemporary scene. His work has an urbane humour, intellect and social comprehensiveness, allied to a finely-honed technical skill, that is only too rare these days. Like Rowan Williams, Grey Gowrie has led a largely public life (company chairman, Cabinet minister, Chairman of the Arts Council of England, and Provost of the Royal College of Art).

The Italian Visitor carries much of this public gravitas in its content, and is a relief from much self-obsessed, solipsistic work. Much of his craft he has learned from Robert Lowell, but his style is distinctive, uniquely his own, demonstrating that emancipated and tolerant and sceptical spirit so much berated (wrongly) by D. H Lawrence (amongst others). His mature style is a narrative one, based upon fictional techniques, a process he says he learned from a study of modern American poetry. In his Editorial to the 'U.S. Poetry Special Issue' of *Agenda* (1976), for instance, he writes (positively) of a contemporary poetic 'application of interests and techniques associated with fiction', and quotes Robert Lowell approvingly on Elizabeth Bishop's work, that it embodies 'the descriptive openness found in the Russian novelists'.

Gowrie's verse endorses the voice of 'an ideal exasperated citizen' (as he expresses it) rather than the self-entrapped obsession of 'the exasperated psyche' of a poet like John Berryman, for example (though still admiring the latter's work). *The Italian Visitor* evokes this critical stance, and properly embodies the difficulty of writing poetry in an age of criticism – the age is scientific, after all, and seems to prefer prose to poetry. Gowrie, like Williams, sets himself to oppose this utilitarianism, remembering that tradition cannot just be trampled upon. In his essay on R S Thomas (both writers appear to have learned much from the Welshman's poetry) he argues that 'the actuality of the here and now is a thin topsoil only, of stored dreams and knowledge'.

The public spirit of Grey Gowrie's poetry, however, in its narrative drive, differs significantly from Rowan Williams' in its concentration on a secular inheritance. He argues that 'existential appreciation of life through art, and an ability to participate ritualistically in life by means of art, is the alternative offered to an untenable religion as well as to nihilism and despair'. One cannot see Dr Williams endorsing that. But this is perhaps to take things too far. Wallace Stevens (an avowed atheist) still believed in the 'Necessary Angel' of the Imagination, and although Osip Mandelstam (to take a rather different case) could write of 'the dead crystal vault of heaven' he could also speak elsewhere of 'the marvellous charity of Christianity, its imaginative release into freedom'. Somehow, in all poetry that matters, these private and public interests interact.

The Italian Visitor is divided into six sections (a series of Pindarics on some Greek friends, amenable and lively cameos; a homage to Eugenio Montale — clearly 'The Italian Visitor' of the title -- which I think is a tour de force, and the best thing in the book; some very moving lyrics based on the Portuguese fado style; a lament for a lost London in 'Kensington Vespers'; some light verse commemorating friends present and past; and a very touching Memoir on Robert Lowell). There are five prose sections to the book which indicate that Gowrie is equally fine at writing prose as he is verse, sections filled with a similar humour, wisdom and wit. Two 'imitations' -- of 'Syria' by Montale (particularly poignant given current circumstances) and 'The Sisters' by Rimbaud also show him to be a talented translator. Gowrie's version of 'Syria' appears to me more successful than George Kay's (in his Penguin edition of Montale) for instance, in its powerful lyricism. It is tightly constructed and crafted, nearer to the spirit of the original:

> The ancients say poems
> are a ladder to God…
> I knew it was so that day
> you gave my voice back to me,
> when goats broke loose from somewhere
> to slaver on thorn or marram
> while clouds lost their bearings
> and sun and moon exchanged
> unearthly looks with each other,
> and our car conked out, and only
> an arrow, a scrawl on stone,
> blood red, as if written in blood,
> pointed us on our way
> by road to Aleppo.

Gowrie has recognised the full significance of 'the arrow' here, referring as it does back to the arrow of love symbolised by the eel ('l'anguilla' – 'eel, torch, lash,/arrow of love on earth', 'l'anguilla, torcia, frusta,/freccia d'Amore in terra') in the poem of that title by Montale. 'An arrow', as Montale has described it in an interview, 'it would seem, that comes from other spheres, a religious interpretation of the world'. The eel symbolises the determined drive of love and of the spirit ('The complexities of mire and blood' as Yeats phrased it, or Pound 'That the universe is alive'). The 'arrow' in 'Syria' suggests a similar attempt to ascend to the realm of Love (though always, at the same time, being dragged down to the earth). Gowrie allows the importance of this poem and its significance to his 'Italian Visitor'.

Gowrie is not afraid to tackle multiple genres (elegy, ode, lyric, epigram, satire, ballad, song, lament) often in their severest rhyming forms, which indicate his seriousness as a writer and the depth of his poetic invention. A sense of history and necessary irony keep him rooted within the English tradition (even if he is writing of Greece, Ireland, Wales or the States), qualities too often lacking in today's literature. His is a social poetry we don't often hear now, far removed from an almost ubiquitous solipsism or self-pitying angst. Alienated hand-wringing is not for him. He wants to put society back on the map. I like his complicated sophistication (his evocations of friendships with Tom Stoppard, Francis Bacon, Robert Lowell, and so on). He is not struggling to be transcendent; he is calmly recognising the limitations of existence and the glories that reside therein – the beneficences of friendship and trust, exploring (as he puts it in his fine essay on R. S. Thomas) 'the intellectual weather of the time'.

In their separate ways, Rowan Williams and Grey Gowrie show us it is possible to bring a public voice to the writing of poetry, at a time when it sometimes seems only of marginal interest.

Tony Roberts

Experiencing Time

Stewart Conn: *The Touch of Time: New and Selected Poems* (Bloodaxe, 2014)
James Harpur: *Angels and Harvesters* (Anvil, 2012)
George Goode: *This Moment Is Gone* (georgewgoode@yahoo.com, 2014)

Stewart Conn's *The Touch of Time* is a welcome and substantial (222 pages) gathering from ten books of poems published over fifty years. One follows Conn's verse as autobiography. Recurrent themes include his delight in daily serendipities, his love of rural ways and his recognition: *timor mortis conturbat me* (the fear of death disturbs me). It is not without coincidence that Conn quotes this popular medieval phrase since, like the fifteenth century Scottish poet William Dunbar who famously used it in 'Lament for the Makars', Conn is himself a poet and maker. What we like about him is how closely he watches, remembers and then retells.

A third of the way into the book we find several poems animated by the fear of mortality. On a trip to Kibble Palace with his children, in 'Return Visit', the poet acknowledges 'time's destructiveness', 'that what's lost/ is within myself' and that 'What future there is, is theirs.' 'Tremors' begins with children by the train tracks and ends:

> Though the end is known,
> there is nothing for it
> but to keep listening…

Even love may not be enough to compensate. 'Arrivals' wonders 'whether being together/ enlarges or diminishes grief.' The source of Conn's concern is his compassion. In 'Before Dark', musing on a photo he explains, 'I cannot bear/ the thought of what loved-ones may suffer./ This is partly what drives me to poetry.'

This preoccupation notwithstanding, these are not gloomy poems. Another characteristic is their *joie de vivre*. The beauty of rural Scotland ('a rurality stoutly asserted') and the hard as flint life led there is recaptured vividly. Conn's passion for fishing and bird watching are insatiable ('You know/ it's an eagle, when you don't need to ask,' his mentor tells him in 'Field Marks'). His love poems written in maturity can be exquisite. Over the years he and his family have visited France and Italy and there are also a number of poems which celebrate Provençal, medieval art and architecture. Then Bonnard's

'The Breakfast Room' is the title poem of one of Conn's finest collections.

The poet's ruminations remain chiefly in the context of Scottish history as well in the senses. His interest in history and myth is balanced by a healthy recognition of contemporary political and class tension ('the city's/ division into haves and have-nots/ never more discordant than today'). These are among the reasons Douglas Dunn celebrated Conn the craftsman as one 'among the indispensable poets' of Scotland.

James Harpur's typically accomplished *Angels and Harvesters* is an exploration of the 'confluence' between the material and spiritual worlds. It is populated by figures from the poet's autobiography and early Christian mystics. In 'Gougane Barra' coins buffed by the shallows of the lake 'keep lit, and hard, the faith behind/ The spinning moment of each wish.' This longing for spiritual meaning is at the heart of the collection.

Fittingly, in poems of heightened awareness, the imagery alternates between the lush ('leaves that drop/ Like bits of flame or scraps of gold') and the rugged ('A day the colour of old chewing gum'). The autobiographical poems are affecting ('Dormitory' and 'Monte Cassino in Kerry'), the mythopoeic powerful. In 'The Removal' a deceased neighbour knocks:

> But what his message was I did not know
> Unless he did not want to be alone
> In darkness, silence, cold, and so had swum
> Towards our lights, towards the nearest home

One admires the drama of the Horatian 'A Churchyard Ghost in West Cork' and the lyrical 'Christmas Snow' with its Joycean echo.

The book's second part bears the title poem. While we strive and yearn for transcendence, angels walk unseen amongst us, leaving the world:

> Without ceremony
> Unless it was
> The swish of scythes
> The swish of scythes

This spiritual yearning is teasingly irretrievable in 'The Pram Pusher's Tale', where Harpur writes of the baby 'Almost remembering paradise':

> There's nothing she can do but look,
> Receive the light and wonder at the wonder,
> The fluent universe of colours;
> For everything flows

In shapes and textures, shades and brilliance
Which have no names, significance.

Grace is hard-earned. The Christian theologian Origen castrates himself ('unbearable the stench/ Of ripeness in the groins'). The fourth century monk, Evagrius Ponticus ('Deserted') wrestles maddingly with temptation. In 'Sinner' we learn of Marguerite Porete agonising death, accompanied by the self-justification of her torturers. In the powerful 'Jacob Boehme's Revelation' the mystic lies in bed with his coarse wife ('Their two worlds back to back') wondering how he can articulate his vision.

However, *Angels and Harvesters* is bookended by affirmative images. In the opening poem, a translation of Rilke's 'Herbst'('Autumn') all is falling: 'And yet there's One who keeps this falling/ From falling farther, endlessly, gently, in his hands.' In the excellent last poem 'Winter Tree', which concerns the seventeenth century conversion of the worldly Brother Lawrence, we recognise grace in the gift of renewal:

Life can never be extinguished;
Bled cold and starved of light it waits,
And waits, for the right unrolling season.

This Moment Is Gone is an outstanding collection of poems privately published by an American poet living in Europe. In a wide range of forms and moods, Goode's poems seek to capture those ephemeral moments of recognition when we let the full force of the world in to enlarge our understanding of the self and human reality. The fifty-eight poems combine sophisticated conceptualized images and graphic physical metaphors to unearth insights into our experience of love, time and death.

The prose poem 'North of the Future' openly speculates on possible escape routes out of the linear concept of time that has dogged us from Aristotle to our current technological age with its mindless mantra of 'progress'. 'We have let the mind get beyond us, a perfect stranger in our midst.' There must be, the poem suggests, a more fruitful way of rethinking our materialist notions of time and the human condition.

Hence Goode explores the mind's elusiveness. The book's opening poem, 'The Second Self', characterises his vision as an odyssey, a necessary pursuit:

Suddenly you are still sitting there
when someone in you has gotten up
and walked out, slamming the door

while 'In the Chestnut Trees' he likens the mind's activity to the natural world: 'A hawk, the mind, the way it swoops and feeds'.

Surrealism and subversive humour are successfully deployed throughout, particularly in the love poems, which reveal a touching and playful innocence. 'Feedback' begins:

> The last time I said anything to you
> you fell into a fountain to join the pennies
> and green waters covered me head to foot.

A number of poems are addressed to 'you' (the divided self or the loved one). Yet the beauty of love – 'That coming out of ourselves into another's eyes' – comes in part precisely from its limits in time. As the poet expresses it in 'The Necessary Error':

> Just as the answer is always coiled and hidden
> in the question, so the uncertainty of our love
> signals implicitly its beginning and its end.

The world and the mind co-exist as one reality in *This Moment Is Gone*. 'Autumn Prelude' conveys something of the Virginian poet's sensuality:

> Even at midday,
> under a full sun, the light has a density
> which seems to envelop, like cellophane,
> the dim din of the crickets deep in their fields,
> while at dusk you can actually feel
> the cold months waiting in the wings,
> curling the broad leaves of summer up
> toward the face of a hard, lean moon.

In 'The Blue Mountains', which ends Goode's collection, he returns to 'these blue friends' which have defined his limits. Here, finally, the world and mind come together as an image of life's impenetrability and beauty:

> The movement of thought is that of a ray of light,
> of sudden mercurial revelation, and the trace left
> is a poetry made of words as unknowable as stones.

Eva Salzman

Isabel,

met first through your dark and handsome
Latinate father so strangely
ignorant you were missing,

it was my calling to bear bad news,
muse-like draft the armies
made of no more than two minds:

a father's mind, my mind
turned to times of a plane's arrival
since on that plane I knew there came

Isabel herself, the very missing one
not missing at all, and never was (jokes
of Isabel on a bicycle aside)

making no sense, except you're each
and every doled-out part in the cast
in the play in the dream

of Isabel, our very missing one.
Maybe it was the Argentinian tinge
of the father's fractured English

or how it was he didn't know.
Somewhere here's a duplicitous one.
Still, he wore his worry well

with furrowed brow. We scan
the online schedules, and don't
those going and gone planes

conjure more of the missing, lost
loved ones. Isabel, I invented you
and I had to save you too.

Hilary Davies

New Year at Aberaeron

I met my friend as we walked by the shore,
Arm in arm with his lover,
Her white-gold hair flying and tracking the wind.
All four we trod at the turning year
On the shingle-shod ground. In my ear
Was the whip and roar of the shearing sea.
We crossed over the bridge of the harbour
With the sun at our back.
                  Ah, my husband,
Let me cup your face with my fingers
By the bright houses and the shouting children
Out on the land's ledge, hung on time's edge
Where Scorpio with her white arms
Flies up into the twilight,
Where the world's great arc wheels
And the souls of the darkening boats
Hanker for the sea.

Sometimes still as in a dream

Sometimes still, as in a dream, you come to me,
Favourite, mercurial uncle, bouncing that admired loquacity
Back and forth all afternoon with my father,
Exulting in visits to Bayreuth, Bergonzi at the Met.
And the largesse of your library, dispensed without afterthought –
'You like it? Then have it!' – embossed Hans Andersens,
First editions, Utrillo, Bonnard, Ceri Richards watching from the walls.
I'm older now that you were when you died.
When did I first discern a straining, an agitation –
Remember the Steinway sent back peevishly after just one assay?
A kind of madness in the talk, as if the talk were action
Or a sanctuary from sirens calling in the deep.
The silence, black dog, the curtains closed at noon
And we, uncomprehending, turned back at your door.
So down the years the pattern, a threnody of envy,
Of being passed over, colleagues' perfidy,
Of all you had not achieved.
Finally, dark things said between brother and brother,
Your wife's head against a wall.
No children. No consummated marriage.
Too strong the claw raking you back to the hissing fireside
Where son and mother reciprocally egged,
Altercated, tore at the fabric of each other's soul.
Each month you swore you'd never again give her
The chance and each month once more
You'd drive the valleys' claustrophobic road
To meet her. All this I saw,
And how for you it ended – my favoured, exotic uncle
Who wrote books on Satie and Poulenc and the leitmotif in Wagner –
After thirty years still the icy shock of Severn water
The horizon unstable, slipping,
Your watch laid carefully by the bedside.
How it looms now, your prodigious codicil:
In your papers no will but a diary
Where in ash you wrote your heart's longing
For a soul woman, wifely counsellor, sweetest of bedmates,
And so begins the first understanding:
That the impossibility of loving begets despair,
And despair kills.

114

Adam Feinstein

Transfusion

In Hotel Senator on Madrid's Gran Vía
I dreamed I was tangled in tubes, handing out life
to my son lying beside me with his lop-sided smile
and the red, sweaty flop of his Beatles haircut.
Or rather,

not life, but the gift of language
to a boy who was crippled
when he lost his speech to autism
at three.

'Which of your seven tongues do you wish to donate?'
the doctor asks from the foot of the bed.
'Spanish – it flows more freely
than English, despite what Borges said.'
I watch a frown ripple on the registrar's face:
'Was he a doctor, this Borges?'

So did the operation make amends?
Would Johnny and I talk like friends?
Somnium interruptus.
Reality's a brute: back home
my gentle boy's still mute.

Copihue

Red *campana*, aphemic,
yet speaking to me now
from the yawn of your mouth.
We're joined by chance: they named you
Chile's national flower
on my birthday.

The Mapuches say you are a tear
shed by warriors
in the aftermath of battle.

But you wage your own war.
You face extinction as you cower
in the damp green bramble
scattered over the mountainside
like clothes cast off
in the heat of lovemaking.

Cling on, copihue.
Cling on, my twin,
in the crease of the *cordilleras*.

Omar Sabbagh

The Salvaging

Yas, Kensington, London

Imagine a fisherman with an infinite net:
His little grey boat, posed, like an infinite bet
Against a sea's wide slurs, her echolalia...

Out of all the fey rhapsodies and masks
The uncaught fish finds his focus, his home
And the spindly fern-pattern before his
Spindly heart, like ribs like fast
empty wishes,
His slim and slippery task:
to be a fish was always daft...

But the bone-thin fisherman, less the kisses
Of some mastered art, turns riled and vicious,
Stark,
a poverty facing the patent riches
Of the glittering, safe, mislaid, dispersed

Fish among fishes...

The Reality of it

Has been a flying dinosaur's wing
Found in the muddy earth, a deep shilling
From the gold standard of yesterday.

Has been the privacy of a well-lit play,
The boards treaded by walking flames,
Ratty pigeons in the scale of things.

Has been the door through which a sire
Goes wedded to a duck, makes a liar
Out of love, makes a liar a liar.

Has been the whole of Africa in
The sweaty palm of an Indian,
Some such transient confusion.

Has been too many clocks to fit
The wall of a reading room, the sins
Of learning, deep, like a covert kit

In a battle raging over all but
That everything which ends and begins
Again and again – as friendship wins.

Has been the torture at the spine
Of a bacterium, or a viral portent in
A Eucharist of wreckage, half-spelt signs.

Has been the major tenor of a life
In which no vehicle is quite
Good enough

To make sense of this bloody mire
In which blood-cells go cheap and for hire –
A cock-up, overall, too much wrong for the lair

Of one beholden man, beholding
The same – and the thick, grisly maze of fear
Through which he scurries: golden / unfolding.

A Dear Friend Grieves

For Patricia McCarthy

Foursquare,
The muscles taut with her loving,
There was nothing
Trojan or double or troubling
About the foursquare mare...

And there was no horsing around
In that companionship: a bond,
A deep and edgeless bond...
Ripped now with sorrow,
Ripped now

By wailing tears, riven, she rows
Whitewaters without sound.

Abegail Morley

Fish wife

The woman who's not my mother has wave-wrinkled skin,
fingers red from filleting fish, dragging knives along their backs,
scales sticking like stars. Her palms are snagged by bones,
broken ends of warp, the pulp of her fingers painful, swollen.

The woman who's not my mother doesn't quail when she cuts off
the head, doesn't flinch as she detaches the stomach, doesn't blink
at the yield of flesh that slides on the plate. She prises open clams
with ease, rinses her oyster-shucker's hands in harsh water.

The woman who's not my mother dries them down her apron
the start of a song trembles on her lips – a secret yearning
twists in her belly, shifts like a shoal of fish skimming
the surface of the water their tails shimmying in sunlight.

Pause

So he told me that by speaking fast
his sadness couldn't catch him –
he'd leave it behind on some highway,
its breath quickening in the verge
but the urge to carry on didn't leave him.

He kept running up streets,
lights at crossings blinking amber
mouth wordlessly moving
up and down and from a distance
it looked like he was saying *'because, because'*.

I checked the back of his head,
watched the yank of his neck
pull itself into a brisk arc
and it was like he was dying at high speed
his mouth too hungry for words.

And when a part of me let him go
he slowed down and a stitch
in his stomach calmed to an incantation,
and he dropped his hand into mine.
I wanted to say *'because, because'*. But couldn't.

The Oncology Community

Here, where the lights flick on early
and the squeal of wheels is like a bird's
throat bolted – every blip on the monitor
is a held breath he traps in his mouth,
daren't release, in case it's his last.

You're here again caught at the edge
of the glass struggling to get free.
Your scales pool like mercury over
each wing, their pattern unique.
I exhale, gift my breath to you who are
almost too tired to flap in the wind.

Mark Harris

for Miller

i

The One

Rain comes in off the estuary,
cascading, scattering dark coral colours
over the waters' surface.
Closer, the rings are separating
and disappearing, each different, endless.
If this rain drop is the only rain drop,
what about this one
pushing down into the waters skull
until it gives
and is swallowed, engulfed, consumed.
Absorbed in the immensity.

ii

Holes

Nothing but darkness,
A blanket hidden beyond kindness;
Unthinkable.
In my dream a stream enters an immeasurable ocean and evaporates.
Do you hear the leaves the wind tears
from the wilderness?
Autumn's guttural gasp.

When light stopped pouring we saw grown-ups come out into the road
and stuff the holes with made up stuff.
I am wondering, from where you are – can you see
these dark reeds coalesce into evening?
Juniper moons ring bright the deft light of a fox's eye
in which berries bloodied black hold back the taste
of the end of the world?

One howl and then nothing.
Even this silence is ridiculous.
Is there anything beyond this sounding and placing of things
In the world?

I have seen a tree burning from the inside out
yet remain un-hollowed, just glowing with light –
A light cut loose and unbreakable.

One day I imagine an orchard at the bottom of the river
And fruit, *real* fruit
inside the core of which
an ocean will whisper your name.

iii

Ions

The light stretches out on the estuary mouth, thin and vaporous.
Kindling on the wind somewhere trees soughing.
Stars walk in our shoes and leave no trace.
All my arms are falling, behind me a child walks picking them up.
You have so many the child smiles
walks off with them to the fire.
You won't need them now.
No, I don't.
Don't need anything. Not arms, mouth... nose.
Not even love.
Connect me to this... Anchor me in the drift of ions that spill forward
beyond oblivion
to the hushed harbour, shushing us to sleep.

Walter

You told me there were fields in heaven, but did
not say they would heal
this void.
You showed me your hand, but did
not let me grasp
its meaning.

Until,
driving back, red lights receding... I sensed if I speeded up
I might almost leave the world
like a gift on the dashboard
for someone else to unwrap.

Night Frog

You came out of darkness
condensing an empty hand
into love.

We live in hotels which grace the evening sky.
At night frogs rush into our room
singing amongst the reeds
about a breeze beneath the moons white rose
whose tears
deepen the darkest ocean.

Dream Lizard

Each night the dream lizard returns through my backyard door.
From the five corners of an outraged world
it speaks of rivers of people
and a dark awareness which taught it its name.

Tonight it comes scuttling across the porch saying it's unravelled
the heart of a silent desert.
Up to the back door it drags its belly with a bush tied to its tail.
It brings a vast thirst and no answers.

It tells me that out in the dust the sun is grooming fields of blossom.
That deep inside cherries are lies not stones.

Stuart Pickford

The Fischer Defence

At six, his sister bought him a set
from their candy store in Brooklyn.
At thirteen, in pullover and cords,
he won the Game of the Century,
slapping the game clock still.

He poisoned pawns, snared
magnetic fields of bishops.
He'd rather a rook than a thumb.
All the pieces were his friends
in the machine. Rhyme with reason.

The Russians drummed their fingers,
humph-ed every move, donned
shades so he couldn't see
the kings in their narrow eyes,
even paid a shrink to spook

him out. But he just picked
the defence that'd bear his name
out of the air: Bk4. Chess
was his mother tongue. Now
he only wore hand-made suits.

'The game plays out the truth,'
he told Nixon as he ruled
the world of black and white.
'There's no escape': I stare,
crush the board into shape.

Ruth Bidgood

Ash

... if thou wilt, remember ...
                (Christina Rossetti, 'When I am dead')

ash on the wind
walk away
say only, This
is like her touch
brushing by
asking nothing

ash on the stream
walk away
say only, This
is like her love
a flowing song
wordless

Linda Benninghoff

Thanatopsis

She must not have come here
to contemplate death, the way
I contemplate winter
as it approaches,
the trees shrugging off leaves,
the grass losing its color,
a paleness everywhere.
the earth turning over
in its mind whether to go on.
But this robin must have come
for her memories,
the branches of the dogwood
forking out in the breeze,
the silver leaves touching,
the small eggs in the nest,
the sky-colored eggs pushing open,
the fledglings who could hoist
themselves from limb to limb,
not quite lifting their wings,
unfettered by age or disappointment,
bearing their parents dreams with them,
as they left her to fly.

William Oxley

Sad Horse

Sad horse
Immobile as a velvet Buddha
We gaze at one another
Who do not know altogether
What it is we are tethered to.
Your eyes are unreachable summers
Of stillness –
But what do you think of mine?
Across the rugged pinioning of a stone
What do you see?
Me
Or more than me?
Well I'll tell you this –
You fine man-broken thing –
I do not know why I feel
About you, sad horse,
As I do
But it's something we share
I am sure.

Tess Jolly

Diagnosis

With all eyes locked on me furled
in the surgery chair in boots and baggy clothes,
the weighing scales' needle shuddering back to zero
and someone talking about the avoidance
of mealtimes, food stashed in cupboards,
the bloom of fine hair on my back and inescapable cold,

I squinted past the doctor's frown and saw you
drumming black lines across the horizon.
Bone-shadow, skeleton moon, echo of the slowed beat
breaking through me, you uncoiled the rope I climbed
blood banging and everyone begging me back,
pressed your mouth to the hot frill of my ear
and crooned to voices chanting in my skull.

On better days I risk looking at the noose dangling
on our terrace, the coat I disappeared in flapping from the line,
my mother planting seeds in the hushed garden
where my teeth-torn fingers snagged on air.

Simon Royall

Helping Out

There was no help to give. A bed for him,
a nurse and a drip and a morphine pump,
nothing of any more use than the organs
returning less of him with every beat.
Powerlessness, never busier, swapped his bed pans,
his pillows, brought tea and gentle jokes.
I marvelled at these energies, bedside,
Cheyne-Stokes breaths their fresh air.

At last, I was joining in. But we can't return
a parent's hugs, Christmases, birthdays,
pecks goodnight, words with bullying teachers;
can't have words with doctors whose fault it's not.
Can't tweeze out tumours, as once they did splinters,
our love become our genius – all we can do

is what they did: hold a hand. Nonsense,
his said. I felt it reassuringly hold mine.

Ruth O'Callaghan

Safari

I have left linen bleaching in a white sun
by an inlet with its slack of winter water

where a heron breaks free from brittle light.
Skin tightened with cold desires the code

of touch. Unregarded, the curvature of trees
bears the mark of previous snows, grass

shrivelled, the earth bitten: winter-ravenous.
Winter-ravenous, I will arrive: my feet bare.

Narrative

Narrative? There is no narrative. Unless you mean
the mice-scratch of voices rising from the reeds'

silty bed or the latent lick of water rimming the bank
from a rower already beyond the curve of the river.

Yet ever, as the last harsh of the late returning crow,
deep-locked, shackles the evening, there remains,

unresolved but latched in re-arrangements of light, air,
stealth, in a conspiracy of shadows, such a hunger

for the unremembered that even a midge or squall of dust
recalls maps of countries no longer named and those

who have no purchase trace, with naked eye, the plane's
arc prinked in the sky like stars in a child's colouring book.

Martin Burke

The Ieper Road

The road ended
In a shimmery haze

Curling to white mist
Over the neat cemeteries

Ieper: old roads and sentential trees
But new roads also

Leading us into
The declensions of history

Which I pronounced
As if it was a blessing

Gleaned from
The names of light

Where old roads and new roads
Narration and mist

Formed the substance
Of our longings

For the sunlit dialogues

Mark Blayney

Two Saturdays

This morning a hundred years ago
you say you are leaving.
In lieu of a reply I shower
and leave a trail of footprints on the carpet
that after breakfast has gone.
I open your wardrobe and ask the clothes
swaying absently inside what went wrong.
They shrug at me, surly, not wanting
to reply while you are not here.

Most have gone now and I see
unexpectedly pale wood at the back.
You ring the bell, which seems surreal,
and the remaining clothes you don't wear very often
are pulled out briskly and laid across your arm.
I watch the dead pupas of weddings,
work functions, early dates and the first time
you came home with me, dance
away with you down the hallway.

Julie Mellor

Reflection

See, in one man's face, the tithe of years,
his eyebrows hung with dust, sleeping bats
folded in their wings behind his eyes.

See, in the map of his skin, how the gaps
have been filled in, how woodworm
has eaten into his heart until it has crumbled away.

The line between his lips is sealed like lead,
the furrow of his brow grained like oak,
and where the wires of his beard have fused

there is the smell of burning,
and where the rivet in his earlobe has widened
the space, look through, see the world turning.

Not Yet Houdini

That day you realised you could bring things up,
not the old country, you'd put that to rest
along with its religion, no, the day you found out
that the gullet was a muscle you could train,
swallowing a key on a length of thread,
a diet of unlocking until you could bring it back
at will. The trick then, behind the screen,
wasn't a contortion of the wrists or dislocation
of shoulder blades,
                                but like an awkward kiss,
the key regurgitated, held between your lips
to turn the lock no matter where you'd find
yourself in the years ahead: a sealed milk churn,
a vat of sand, the belly of a whale
washed up on Boston beach.

Michael McCarthy

A Better Place

You see it all now in slow motion.
The back-to-backs emptying. The houses
lonesome, then derelict: the roofs coming off
and the walls groaning. You see the cobbled
streets un-cobble, and the fancy stone-faced
retaining wall grow higher and longer, and
below it the dual carriageway shaping out.

Heavy machinery clangs, and at weekends
sits there defiant. Then, on the Monday
Mrs Armstrong's house comes down.
Mrs Armstrong is in a better place
her daughter says, not meaning
that she's dead. Nor is her house.
It's still breathing, somewhere.

Meanwhile the new houses back on
to the park, and the stone-faced wall
is still sturdy though darkened by time.
Forty years, and the carriageway, last time
you drove it had repair signs and machines.
Looks like they're widening it again. You wonder
what Mrs Armstrong makes of it now.

David Cooke

Sounding the Silence: Some recent Irish Poetry.

Mary Noonan: *The Fado House* (The Dedalus Press, 2012)
Eleanor Hooker: *The Shadow Owner's Companion* (The Dedalus Press, 2012)
Vona Groarke: *X* (The Gallery Press 2014)
Paddy Bushe: *My Lord Buddha of Carraig Éanna* (The Dedalus Press, 2012)
Sean Lysaght: *Carnival Masks* (The Gallery Press, 2014)

Mary Noonan's *The Fado House* is a remarkably assured first collection. It gets off to a flying start with 'Keep Talking, Babe', a poem that is both disorientating and dazzling. As in the work of Eiléan Ní Chuilleanáin, that doyenne of Irish poetry and one whom Noonan clearly admires, we are offered little in the way of back story or recognizable context:

> It was his dream to see me through a screen
> With words and music and a cast of dwarves
> Playing card-sharps, hecklers, fire-eaters.
> My only act was to jabber, but I could work it up
> To a howl, and this I did for centuries.

A consummate performance in its own right, 'performing' is essentially what this poem is about and it takes a confident poet to carry it off: 'The beauty of my inflection was enough to catch / The crowd, and when I had them I'd lunge / Between whisper and rant, spinning on plosives.' The impressive poise and headlong rush of Noonan's syntax here is replicated in other pieces early on in *The Fado House*. 'I will Gabble' again plunges us *in medias res,* albeit in a more easily apprehended social context. Out of the blue the protagonist gets a phone call: 'and there you were my heart ripped / from its coat of mail and tap-dancing all over my chest'; while in 'Night Traffic' Noonan's lengthy run-on lines might easily have teetered over the edge into prose or chaos were it not for the controlled flamboyance of her language:

> Into the candle-flame went
> talk of Mexico City and the high-wire circus of Budapest
> and the German outposts of Transylvania and the lure
> of pepper (chilli, paprika) and three bottles of French wine
> and the touch of his hands.

In 'Swallow' there is a similar, if slightly more restrained, forward movement which, somewhat in the manner of Eugenio Montale's *'L'Anguilla'*, evokes a small creature's urge to migrate and the epic journey that lies before it:

Soon she will be darting over miles
of dust tract, past ghost shack and scrub
glancing off rock cacti that do not sink roots
but run feelers lightly over dunes, cup rain
as it slides through spines.

However, impressive as the unfettered élan of such poems may be, the reader would soon grow weary if this were Noonan's only mode. By way of contrast, there are poems such as 'Evening in Muscat', in which the details are quietly noted and a scene is presented cinematically:

The muezzin's cry rings from unseen minarets, incantatory,
unavoidable. Cushions and satellite dishes litter flat roofs,
wind chimes scatter flocks of small parrots.
Cocks crow, night falls quickly.

'The Fado House of Argentina Santos' is another precisely observed poem which makes an interesting contrast with 'Keep Talking Babe'. Structurally, the two poems seem poles apart, yet both are concerned with the role of the artist and the way she expresses herself. Here, we enter the world of the Portuguese *fadistas*, performers *par excellence,* who sing songs of *saudade* or 'longing', a concept as elusive as the Andalucian *duende* or the gospel singer's *soul*: 'Cradling herself in a fringed shawl / she opens her throat and ululates / in broken tremolo for the old dreams.'

Stylistically varied, the fifty five poems of *The Fado House* are also wide-ranging in their geographical locations: from Noonan's family roots in Ireland to the many places she has since travelled: France, Portugal, Germany, The Middle East, India. However, those set in Ireland and inspired by family memories are among the most directly effecting. 'The Turnip' is a beautifully rendered poem which captures *haecceitas* in a way that Heaney or Ponge might well have been proud of: 'big, hairy, yellow *bostoons*, food fit for sows and *banbhs'*. The vegetable then takes on a symbolic resonance as it becomes emblematic of the poet's personal trajectory: 'Warming to your subject, you likened the difference / between the fine French navet and the rough Irish / variety to that between a thoroughbred and a dray'. 'Winter Clothes' and 'No Shoes' point up the poverty of rural Ireland in the 1940s and 1950s, which led to mass migration. This is the subject of 'The Rosslare Train, Fermoy,

August 20, 1956', a poem that Noonan has dedicated to her father, a keen athlete whose foot was spiked the day before he was due to leave: 'It's true this place / couldn't give me a living, but it gave me running / and leaping and playing – a wild boy's life'. Impassioned and vibrant, *The Fado House* is a collection that one can wholeheartedly recommend. It has depth, range, and endless resonance.

Eleanor Hooker's *The Shadow Owner's Companion* is also a début collection from the Dedalus Press. A quieter and less obviously self-assured writer than Noonan, Hooker's poems are introspective and exploratory, drawing the reader into a shadowy world of archetypes, where meanings are frequently inchoate or at best provisional. This is, of course, a high risk project, as Hooker, no doubt, realises, having chosen to place an epigraph from Charles Simic's '*The World Doesn't End*' at the front of her collection: '*My guardian angel is afraid of the dark. He pretends he's not, sends me ahead, tells me he'll be along in a moment*'. The distance that has to be travelled between Hooker's 'life' and her 'work' is emphasised in 'Why':

Why so dark, so negative, about death?
You ask of what I write.

I am a loving wife, devoted mother
And yet none of this in poems?

It's a distance that is also crossed in 'Three Things', the villanelle with which she opens her collection:

Three things I keep secure: my life, my truth, my boys.
As I contemplate the surface of the lake,
Three things I long to lose: my doubts, my fears, their lies.

Although the villanelle is frequently a vehicle for light verse, Hooker achieves an impressive weight and expressiveness by employing, predominantly, lines of twelve syllables. Her neat exposition, with the two repeated lines mirroring each other across the clear surface of the lake, is concise and effective. Almost immediately, however, we are plunged into a world of subconscious fears and uncertainties prowled by the pike, a Hughesian predator that features in several of Hooker's poems: 'Through underwater gloom, pike eyes / Find me, their torn mouths lipstick-stained.' Fixed forms are frequently used to good effect in this collection, helping the poet to contain her more visionary impulses and giving her plenty of scope to create musical effects. 'Cell Phone' is another successful villanelle: 'I cup your voice to my ear. / Your warming breath against my skin, / You hold my hand though you're not here'; while 'Cold Snap' and 'Songs of the Sea' exploit the musicality of the pantoum. In the former a pike again prowls ominously beneath the surface of a frozen lake:

> I loved it when the world went white.
> The land was hushed and ghost-like.
> Constellations pierced the night light,
> And, deep in the lake, the still pike...
>
> The land was hushed and ghost-like.
> A greedy moon ate up the sky,
> Constellations pierced the night light,
> The anaemic sun was mystified.

In 'Fishing' her appropriation of a nursery rhyme is, perhaps, less assured and otherwise fine poems such as 'Someone Tell Me' and 'Old Harry 'are not enhanced by unnecessary refrains. The former is built around a sequence of three interrogatory stanzas:

> Have you ever noticed how the embossed
> paper, walled in the sick room, is a living, moving,
> breathing thing that absorbs all thought,
> night-time, blood, ash trees, old oaks,
> firsts, lasts, the moon, a parent? How the days
>
> of your life are written on those walls, how this day
> fails to be a blue-lit, sun-skied place?

> *Well have you?*

Echoing each question between the stanzas adds nothing to the poem's overall effectiveness and seems a tad too earnestly insistent; while in 'Old Harry', one of several poems on a maritime theme – which are amongst the best in the book – the impetus of the narrative is, if anything, undermined, by its melodramatic refrain. However, in a début collection, one is entitled to try on masks and experiment with form. In spite of occasional stylistic uncertainties, there is much that is promising here. A helm and Press Officer for the Lough Derg RNLI Lifeboat, Hooker is always impressive when she writes about boats and the sea. 'Recovery' is a moving account of a failed rescue attempt: 'The rhythmic pitch // of our engine's blades is the sound / of

143

hope in tortured air'. 'The Island', a personal favourite and one of the most achieved poems in the collection, is a narrative poised between dream and reality that starts out with the epic assurance of Richard Murphy:

> In this summer heat as I oar us out of depth
> The shoreline shimmers unsteadily, and when the engine coughs
> We are underway at last. The island's trees are lined with birds,
> Heraldic wings outstretched drying in the sun,
>
> A cormorant arboretum.

Yet beyond the poem's convincing actuality, the narrative is cunningly imagined and ends, impressively, on a note of Yeatsian nostalgia:

> To the arhythmic drumbeat from my heart,
> We are rocked asleep inside a dream of *Kibihee* being rocked asleep
> Inside a dream. And when I awake, I'll know it's time.

A writer who is maybe still finding her way, one senses that Hooker has had to work through intractable material as a part of her learning process. She is always at her best when the language is simple and her eye is clearly focused as in these lines from 'Melting Ice':

> The lake froze, froze all the way to
> Clare, a fine bone china plate whose
> glaze cracked when the melt came.

From two poets starting out we move on to Vona Groarke whose debut collection, *Shale*, was published twenty years ago and who, since then, has been one of the most consistently satisfying voices on the Irish poetry scene. Her enigmatically titled new collection, *X*, is her sixth. At first glance, there is much included here that is familiar from previous volumes: domestic interiors and the objects they contain, daily routines, family, and everything else suggested by 'the museum of the ordinary', that memorable phrase from her poem 'The White Year.' In 'Going Out', a poem dedicated to her daughter, she beautifully captures the relationship between them and hints at the passage of time:

> My daughter, heading out on the town in her glad rags,
> laughs a laugh like a floribunda rose pinned in her hair.
> She has so much beauty in her, more than this summer
> evening, in all its frippery. More even, than the sound

of her heels the length of the road, her phone voice
dipping into company, the pooled high talk of her
and her friends slipping through the city's open door.

However, many of the poems in *X* are informed by a sense of unease. Again from 'The White Year': 'A skim of plausible survival / settles on what I do;' in the opening couplet of 'Where She Imagines the Want of Being Alone' she highlights the contrast between the security of 'home' and the uncertain world that lies beyond it: 'A small house. Rooms with white door handles / and a dangerous sky to be trapped in window frames.' '3' is a poem about moving into a new house, a theme which Groarke has explored in previous work, but which seems here to be shaped by changed personal circumstances:

My house of uneven numbers,
of my children's hyphenated lives.
My house of small hours, of voices
a little quieter than they need to be.

Frequently this uneasiness expresses itself in a Wittgensteinian concern to explore the limits of language and discover what is knowable. It's an obsession highlighted in an epigraph from Florian Cajori: '*René Descartes'* la Géometrie (1637) *introduces the use of the first letters of the alphabet to signify* known *quantities and the use of last letters to signify* unknown *quantities'*. Here is Groarke in her prose poem 'Aubade': 'My words gave out: they couldn't stand the depth of optimism. They have acquired holes through which the sense of what I mean slips in. I could say I am lonesome and the words would laugh their tin laugh back at me.' Taking the hint from her Cartesian epigraph, the collection's title poem plays with the various possibilities of a mathematical symbol:

a shape
signifying nothing
but a puzzle of itself...

fused the way lovers are fused
for as long as it takes
to pass through the eye of love
to recover, to egress.

It concludes with an image that is not only powerfully suggestive, but a brilliant materialization of an abstract form: ' I may begin... // to learn how a life may come to rest / on the absence of a life ... // as the blades of a bedroom ceiling fan / come to // a perfectly obvious stop.'

Groarke's metaphysical concerns and her attempts to explore the contingent nature of existence are often moving, but they do, on occasion, tie her up in knots, when syntax is laboured or the words are merely portentous. However, at her best she has lost none of her ability to celebrate life as it is lived moment by moment. Here is the opening stanza of 'The Front Door':

> The sky inside my head grows out
> of a single cell of blue. One minute,
> I'm snicking geraniums and, before you know it,
> there's larks and curlews and a jet-trail
> with no beginning to it unzipping my last thought.

Balanced against 'the contingent darkness' and 'the faithless slippage of things' there is, in 'Midsummer', an intimation of new beginnings: 'All to play for. Yesterday the rain kept hinting / it had something to say'. *X* is a collection shot through with shimmering imagery which is, by turns, elemental or painterly. There are wonderful poems evoking the work of Derain, Monet and Hammershøi and an ambitious set of poems called 'The Garden Sequence' which bring together many of the collection's ontological themes. It is a challenging, but ultimately rewarding collection, which is illuminated by the beauty of its language, or, as Groarke herself expresses it in her poem 'Architecture', by 'words like stones with sunlight on them'.

My Lord Buddha of Carraig Éanna is a new collection from Paddy Bushe, an award winning poet who has written in both English and Irish. It is also his first collection since *To Ring in Silence: New and Selected Poems,* which was published in 2008. A substantial body of work, ranging from brief lyrics and haikus to meditations on landscapes and their spiritual implications, his latest book is a wide-ranging volume in which the poems fall naturally into five sections. There is also, as a bonus, a version of Eibhlín Dhubh Ní Chonaill's classic lament 'Caoineadh Airt Uí Laoghaire' for which Bushe has come up with the Ginsbergian title of 'The Howl for Art Ó Laoghaire.

In the first section the poems are largely set in Ireland and the United States. However, it opens with 'Organ Recital, Norwich Cathedral', a poem hinting at the possibility of transcendence:

> The organ-pipes, sunstruck by the last rays
> Through the high cathedral windows, beamed
> Beyond sin or sanctity, radiating around
> Arches, colonnades and flowering vaults.
> And, secular with sacred, Latinate

With vernacular, the music moved
Eternally within the walls. Bede's sparrow
Would have flown in and never left.

By way of contrast, in 'Swans' the poet achieves a sense of uplift by observing nature: 'The high whirring music of their wings // building to a climax as they rose up / and over the gable, and the whole / House lifted, as if filled with sails.' In 'The Search' he explores a landscape and mythologizes the origins of language: 'He wanted to know what language the river / Spoke at its earliest bubblings, how the brown bog / Inflected its original accent'.

Then, from the bogs and rivers of Ireland, he takes us, in his second section, to the rugged mountains of Nepal, giving ample testimony to his descriptive powers. In 'Votary at Chaudaridara' we see how 'the early morning sun sheds light on the humps / And hollows of the water-buffalo's back, silvering // those Himalayan hips to pewter'. In 'New Moon over Nepal' 'a sickle moon rises / and edges itself against the grain of stars.' However, beyond merely capturing local colour, these are poems that seek new paths towards self-knowledge and enlightenment. In 'Swing' the poet takes part in a local festival and learns that 'everybody's feet ... should leave the earth / during *Dashain*, and walk the air like kites'. Moreover, with their precipitous pathways and terrifying bridges, the soaring heights of Nepal bring home to the poet life's fragility. In 'On Thorung La', a poem in which he addresses his wife on their fortieth anniversary, he comes to realize that true knowledge is always hard won. 'I had a rucksack of tropes for this poem', he tells us, until his 'tropes fell away abruptly into the void'.

In 2010 Bushe edited *Voices at the World's Edge: Irish Poets on Skellig Michael*. The poems which he himself contributed to this anthology are now included in the fourth section of his latest collection, their evocation of early Irish monasticism forming an interesting adjunct to those inspired by Nepali Buddhism. The sequence opens, appropriately enough, with 'Entrance' which points towards an 'otherworldly plenitude'. In 'Illuminated Manuscript' the visiting poet identifies with the Skellig's original inhabitants:

Last night I boiled the young sorrel leaves
I had gathered behind the monastery ...

And although there was also tinned food,
Instant coffee, a solar-powered fridge
And mobile phone reception near the helipad,
For *supper*, read *collatio*,
For *hut*, read *cell* or *scriptorium*...

In 'Skellig Birds', a sequence of haikus describing the numerous species that have made this rock their perch, he employs a form imported from the east that is also reminiscent of the hermit poems and glosses of early Irish literature. East and west also come together in the collection's eponymous central section which personifies a statue of the Buddha that Bushe has placed in his garden overlooking the Atlantic Ocean:

> He has settled in well. Some two
> Or three winters. Stirs himself only
> For the approaching lawnmower. Sinks
> Easily back into where he was.

Wise and absorbing, *My Lord Buddha of Carraig Éanna* is the work of a poet who is plainspoken, eloquent, and movingly authentic.

Finally, we turn to *Carnival Masks* by Sean Lysaght, whose new collection, his sixth, is, like Bushe's, the first he has published since his *Selected Poems* in 2010. A lecturer in the Galway-Mayo Institute of Technology, he has also published a biography of the Irish naturalist Robert Lloyd Praeger. It is not surprising, therefore, that his work is characterized by its meticulous observation of natural phenomena. In the first half of his collection domestic lives are set against a backdrop of the changing seasons. 'Skylarks in January' is a typically contained lyric in which the matter of fact tone of a diary entry is suddenly illuminated by a brilliantly apposite image:

> None since October,
> and now there are four
> calling across the clouds,
> still dragging a grey hawser
>
> that ends in the sea
> after weeks in the links...

As he contemplates this bleak autumnal scene the poet comes to an understated conclusion: 'all love wants – there in the heather – is a nest.' Moving on to February, 'Catkins', is a brief love poem whose final stanza is as simple and affecting as a mediaeval lyric: 'Ah, this is the seed of the wind, / which I scatter for you / wherever you touch or bend / in the bright dew.' Throughout these poems, it is not only Lysaght's undeniable skills of observation that are impressive, but his ability to come up with images that are freshly minted and memorable. In the month of March 'Wind scours the bones of the living;' while in April 'The north-east is an unbidden guest, / a grumpy old man /

whose shed is full of skylarks.' In poem after poem Lysaght homes in on small details, as here in 'Hazelbrook' where 'each hoof-print' is 'a cupful of clearing sky'. A skilled ornithologist, he listens in to unseen jays 'tearing like engines / at the fabric of a winter's day: while 'Five Hawks' is a tour de force in which each predator is sensed via the reactions of their potential prey. Birdlife also features in a moving sequence dedicated to the memory of his father, from whom he learned his love of nature and with whom he studied Praeger.

However, having laid to rest the ghost of his father, Lysaght moves beyond his love of natural history in an impressive sequence of six 'Sonnets to a Tudor Poet'. Exploring the legacy of Sir Edmund Spenser, he revisits the Irish countryside in its historical and cultural context. Taking as his point of departure a jawbone salvaged from a Sixteenth Century massacre, he acknowledges the complexities of history by seeming to mock his own facility:

> Metaphors, no problem. Molars are stones
> to step over the stream of time, the bone
> is an obol under the thumb for Charon –
> journeyman stuff! It does not tell how he cursed
> in Italian; his panic came
> too late to be read back from the bone,
> and yet this must be where my English starts,
> this remnant of a garrison poleaxed.

If Spenser was variously inspired by Gloriana, Ireland and the Italian language, Lysaght's work, in the course of his final pages, is informed by influences beyond the West of Ireland. In 2008 he published a translation of Goethe's *Venetian Epigrams*. Here, in his own 'Venetian Notebook' he follows in his master's footsteps, expressing himself in a more ironic vein: 'When dining in Venice, if you want to be fleeced, / go to the places where great writers used to eat!' This is followed by a translation of Goethe's poem of yearning for the South, 'Do You Know the Land Where the Lemons Grow' alongside three fine versions of Rilke. The collection is brought to a close by several poems in which the panoramas of Southern Europe are in marked contrast to those at home: their 'palette rich / with citrus trees, olive trees, / hibiscus and bougainvillea.' *Carnival Masks* is a very satisfying and immediately accessible collection by a poet with two enviable gifts: his clear eye and an ear attuned to the music of language. Not since I first read the poems of Ted Hughes and Ted Walker, have I been so impressed by a poet's ability to capture and make memorable the minutiae of the natural world.

W S Milne

The Dedicated Spirit: New Poetry

Fiona Benson: *Bright Travellers* (Cape, 2014); **Alyson Hallett**: *Suddenly Everything* (Poetry Salzburg, 2013); **Jim Maguire**: *Music Field* (Poetry Salzburg, 2013); **Frances-Anne King**: *Weight of Water* (Poetry Salzburg Pamphlet Series 10, 2013); **Tim Liardet**: *Madame Sasoo Goes Bathing* (Shoestring Press, 2013); **Abegail Morley**: *Eva and George – Sketches In Pen* and Ink (Pindrop Press, 2013); **Norbert Hirschhorn**: *Monastery of the Moon* (Dar al Jadeed, P.O. Box 11/5222, Beirut, Lebanon, 2012); **Sarah Wardle**: *Beyond* (Bloodaxe, 2014); **William Bedford**: *The Fen Dancing* (Red Squirrel Press, 2014); **Rory Waterman**: *Tonight the Summer's Over* (Carcanet Press, 2013); **Lynne Wycherley**: *Listening to Light: New & Selected Poems* (Shoestring Press, 2014)

The governing motif of Fiona Benson's first collection of poetry, *Bright Travellers*, is childbirth, its pains and joys – the poet follows her daughter's first steps playing halfway down a field, and fearing for the life she has before her, the child acquiring new experiences which cannot be expressed in a rational formula, all written with great sensitivity and tenderness. The book comes highly recommended, and rightly so, by Michael Longley, John Burnside and Michael Symmons Roberts. Roberts writes that 'these are poems of great tenderness but an undertow of violence and loss gives them a hard-won, miraculous quality.' There is a sequence at the heart of the volume based on the letters and paintings of Vincent Van Gogh which represents a palimpsest of her own emotions: 'The times /of clarity and grace are more and more/remote,' but still life provides 'the blazing candour of light,' 'the stars' ecstatic fires.' Here lies the consolation of art, and also the blessings of continuing life.

Suddenly Everything by Alyson Hallett likewise celebrates that which is marvellous but also terrifying at times. She praises the epiphanies of art ('*liber*,' she says, 'means both book and free,' emphasising that natural spontaneity, that spirit which challenges the humdrum routines of living). Her poetry praises 'the book of days – full of faults/and the terrible tenderness of flesh,' and the elemental splendours of the moon, mist, sea, 'wind, rain, storm,' 'rock, a heron, a vein of sap,' 'skin and sun, eye and stone and tree' in almost Pongean elaborateness, digging beneath life's superficies, glimpsing the essence beneath the surface of things, helping us to see such phenomena anew. Penelope Shuttle writes of her richly 'observed intensities… voicing the world in all its richness,' and I think that is just about right.

Jim Maguire's first collection of poetry, *Music Field* is concerned with 'the poignancy of men/shouldering unbearable things,' a world in which too often music, or harmony, is 'swallowed by stone.' The 'hands' here concentrate on one thing only: the playing of the piano, usually to perfection. But there is a terror or darkness to this playing: 'a terrifying expanse' in which often memory lapses and errors occur in a movingly human dimension. The piano playing releases 'a craving', 'the torture-machine' (the piano) 'has been goading you for weeks,' the composition quite often an alienating process, a 'heart-stopping/touch of anonymous hands,' an atmosphere where 'clemency' is only 'bestowed in the silent moments,' *'the language where language ends,'* in 'intimate converse with the divine.' Here we have a true embodiment of the inwardness of things, the terrors of 'the cliffs of the mind' when it yearns for perfection – a spirit 'hazed/with longing' for 'God-hungry silences.' 'The pianist is left with nothing to do but think/stillness, distance...' Maguire writes, far from 'the shadows rising, sinking,' far from 'the gallows stench/in the vault.' The inspiration comes from within, not without, 'the magnificent risks/of a mind shaking loose from outmoded forms,' a spirit determined not to be 'mired in the rutted lanes.' Design here comes from intuition, not from preconception, seeking the hidden effects of music and its effects upon the mind.

Frances-Anne King's pamphlet *Weight of Water* is an interesting collection, Tim Liardet correctly stating on the book-cover that the poems 'strike a beautiful balance between mystery and disclosure, bravery and tact.' There is a crystallizing of emotion and thought here which reminds one of Imagism in the precision of the lines, but with King's own stamp of originality and exactitude: 'the murk of shadows... sifting images through my mind,' 'the tracing of branch-bones against a washed-out sky,' 'the bone-lit morning light' (conveying intimations of death), 'the heart behind the shadow of the lungs,/the armour of ribcage' (on a visit to a medical museum), 'the sound of bodies breathing/through the slow haemorrhage of dawn' (writing of her nursing experiences at Barts Hospital). Death is 'the call of ancient stone,' 'the skeletons of sharks,/ crocodiles in clay,' 'a scattering/of ash in a fireplace,' never far from the surface of things, the dark side of life as Rilke praised it. There is that sense of eternity one finds in Henry Vaughan's poetry, of the binding of life and shadow: 'They will be waiting for you in the garden/ under the Cornus controversa –/its tapered leaves edged creamy white –/perhaps you'll see them through the tiered branches,/their profiles clear against the light.'

Frances-Anne King acknowledges the influence of Tim Liardet in her Foreword to *Weight of Water*, so it is interesting to see her pamphlet complementing Liardet's most recent sequence, *Madame Sasoo Goes*

Bathing. This is his ninth book of poems, and in it he imagines a beast from Antarctica washed ashore on the Indian Ocean island of Mauritius – an enigma that no one seems to be able to solve. The beast, we are told on the dust-cover (Yes! There are still books with dust-covers!) is 'a Francis Bacon nightmare, a product of the upending of nature that is climate change.' The sequence, we are told, was inspired by a reading of Darwin's *Voyage of the Beagle,* and the South Sea paintings of Paul Gauguin, but as a reader I find more of Swift's Brobdingnag in the volume, and a touch of Defoe's Robinson Crusoe – a strange mixture of fantasy and reality. The beast is a type of modern-day Kraken, or Leviathan, rising from the deeps (maybe with a touch of Yeats' 'Second Coming' in mind – 'And what rough beast, its hour come round at last,/ Slouches towards Bethlehem to be born' …), a chiliastic moment for humankind in any case. As might be expected in our murderous age, it is not long before someone shoots the beast, before anyone has had time to analyse or probe its mysteries – it may be that out of a seeming ecological disaster some token of hope has been given to us – but too late, it has been cut down before we can understand it. There is a persistent strangeness to this volume that holds the reader's imagination throughout, the limning of an odd and disconcerting situation which is almost like sci-fi in its effects – a dream of life, rather than life itself, much as in Gauguin's own paintings. It is a difficult poem, but one worth exploring.

Dennis O'Driscoll has argued (in an essay published in *Agenda* entitled 'R.S Thomas and the Poetry of Paintings') that 'the combined wall space of all the world's galleries would not be sufficient to accommodate the poems about paintings written in the last century.' And I think I know what he means. It is a genre that one feels has been more or less over-worked. However, there are exceptions to every rule, and one exception is Abegail Morley's *Eva and George – Sketches In Pen and Brush,* her third collection of verse. It is a poetic account of the painter and satirist George Grosz and his wife Eva Peter in the days of the Weimar Republic, as Nazi power is on the rise – the poems written in the voice of the wife. The poems are finely interleaved with reproductions of Grosz's telling graphic satires, and capture the growing prescience of terror: 'We are like cattle, all of us.// Your body rattles in its core. You rant, tell us all/ you'll go mad with melancholy. Everything/around you is damnable. Now the hospital/ detains you a little longer, declares you unfit.// We are like cattle, all of us.' There are vignettes of 'the monstrous menagerie' of Berlin, the hate mail delivered to Grosz by Nazi sympathisers (all of it anti-Semitic, though he was in fact not Jewish, just adding to the absurdity), 'Black boots beating up the stairs,' 'the cataloguing/of cadavers' before the couple finally decide to emigrate: 'We leave the lung-stabbed air of Germany/ with its infantry soiling the land,/ its demons, dictator and Dachau.'

Grosz, the painter-satirist, wields the horror with his pencil, sketching 'the soon-dead.' The black outline of Grosz's art can be seen inspiring all of the poems in Morley's pamphlet.

Middle Eastern culture is the central subject of Norbert Hirschhorn's *Monastery of the Mooon*, a pan-Arab position which is only too rare today. He praises the Arabic poets who have concentrated on the cherishing of words (*hilal*, 'scimitar against a vermilion sky'; *al-atlal*, 'remembrance'; the origins of 'orchard' and 'paradise' in ancient Persian), a culture which he hopes over time will again find its roots after the internecine struggles of the Middle East have died down, when there is no longer a stream of refugees spilling over the borders, when famine and drought come to an end. The voices of Firdosi, Rudaki, Sa'di, Hafiz, Rumi and Omar Khayyam can be heard behind such lines as Hirschhorn's 'Scimitar moon, a woman's laughter untouched behind/ wood shutters. Under a red tile roof, a house moults from/ within, muffled piano strings'... (from 'Lebanon'). Behind the 'concrete pylon'... 'landfills choked/ with shredded t-shirts and jeans,' 'the growl of turbines' (and the car bombs) he can still hear the ancient love-songs and prayers of the past. Far from 'the human ruckus' 'for just a few beats of a pulse in my ears,/ a peace embraces our street./ The men who pray raise up their palms./Soon the sun will warm the stones'; 'Let us repair to olive trees, date palms, evergreens… auroras, mint-green scintillae/ heralding daybreak's pale blush,/ proving our beneficent world.' His poems tell us there is always room for hope, even in the middle of catastrophe.

Beyond is Sarah Wardle's third collection of poetry, a sequel to *Fields Away* and *Score!* As in the previous books, London provides the setting for many of her poems, a symbol, as the book-cover tell us, 'of the harsh realities of life and yet also the human love and compassion we can experience in everyday responses.' Each poem is a cameo of London life: an interview with an interesting shrink in a somewhat claustrophobic setting, the vicissitudes of teaching and of marking university scripts, encounters with 'freshers' and with the homeless, hotels serving greasy breakfasts, Prufrockesque 'rooms like stage sets saucepans simmer/ to boiling point, while double beds at night/ lie facing walls, it's each blue light/ that draws you in, tellies that flicker/like gas flames, glimpsed through open windows,' the desolation of week-ends, the hopeful exorcise of desperation through Citybreaks, 'the cold abyss' of loneliness, depression, loss of self, 'suffocating in the throng/ that marches down The Strand as one,' 'the city's solitude' 'when the day is grey as pencil lead,/ and sky on the verge of sieving rain, and your mind soaked but still stained… when hope slips from your hands like soap.' There is a Blakean epiphany of 'the battered child crying himself to sleep,/ the heroin-user shooting his fix,/ the troubled woman jumping into the street,/ will be ferried not on the Thames, but Styx.' However, the bleakness is often redeemed in Wardle's work, and she often seeks (and finds) the hidden life of nature (even in London) and registers its effects upon her mind. There is a seeking of religious values, but not dogmatically, in her poetry. She finds peace in the presence of horses, in her flying lessons, and the continuance of life: house martins 'too busy to be aware they're alive', 'Morning/ sun is enough, the pace of eight o'clock/ pavements, the urgency of Victoria Station,' 'midsummer's radiance', 'a stillness of body and of mind.' 'Something in me says begin to trust,/ even if I'm not the type to pray.' The solitude is broken, if just for a moment, and somewhere a housewife 'swoops to the ironing/ and she starts to sing.' On first reading this book I thought the poems were somewhat artificially arranged, but on closer inspection I can see each poem surprises the reader with the inter-mixedness of things, how joy and despair are never far apart.

As in previous collections, William Bedford's *The Fen Dancing* concentrates on his childhood memories of Lincolnshire, but extends his landscape back historically to evoke the fens around the time before the outbreak of the First World War, a time of peace and community: '*a horde of children skreeking to the beck,/young women twisting aprons/through gnarled fingers,/horses shrouded by a gadder of flies.*' He is intent on rescuing the dialect from oblivion (there is one poem, somewhat strangely, written in Scots, 'after Hugh MacDiarmid') writing of 'winter's crizzling grind,' 'Elizabeth wouldn't be mithered to listen,' 'The village gossips called her warm,/ and *mawk* behind her back,' 'nowt to do w'maudlin', preserving the 'Lincolnshire vowels' he cherishes so much. The vocabulary at times is not so far removed from John Clare's Northamptonshire. There are other poems concerned with travels abroad, his favourite artists, poets and musicians (Whitman, Frank Lloyd Wright, Shelley, Sidney, Miles Davis, John Adams, Jack Kerouac, Allen Ginsberg, and so on) which bring variety to the volume. Like them, he finds 'Imagining is the only way to survive,' poetry's consolation transcending 'the mad distress' which is ours. There is a passing acknowledgment to Philip Larkin's 'the Whitsun Weddings' in 'a slow stopping train trundling a bleak landscape' (in 'John Adams in America') and a wonderful translation of Book I: IV of Ovid's *Amores*. The book is worth savouring for the translation alone.

Rory Waterman, a former young *Agenda* Broadsheet poet, writes of Lincolnshire too in his debut collection, *Tonight the Summer's Over*, but the background here is more urban and more depressed than William Bedford's. There are a number of poems concerning the break-up of his parents' marriage and the bitterness that ensued, vignettes of week-end visits by his father, outings with his stepfather, and so on, that are contemporary in outlook. There are poems also about visits to Scotland, Wales, the Faroe Islands and Ireland which provide a balance of material to the volume. But he too, like Bedford, is drawn to the countryside: 'suddenly, the shattered hedges, ancient copses,/ our huge ruined villages, give way as/dimpled fields tilt to the Fen/and the treeless otherworld begin'... Rory Waterman writes on the edge where 'keen-eyed observation and immediately graspable shades of feeling' (the words are Alan Jenkins') balance precariously, holding despair and anguish at bay.

It is rare to come across a body of poetry abounding in so much 'love' and 'beauty'. Lynne Wycherley's *Listening to Light* is full of just this. Not only does the reader 'listen' to the 'light' in her delicate, deft poems, but the poems themselves all carry a lightness linked to an ease of speech; they shine with light and air all around them. Honed, sparse, they are painterly, and resemble the 'Chinese brushstrokes// magnetic distances/ hollowed in light' in the poem 'Toward Evening, Holme Fen'. They also demonstrate an interestingly original use of unusual words which expands and renews the English vocabulary. Impressively wide-ranging in both theme and place, the poems take us all over England and Scotland; Blake, Constable, John Clare, Julian of Norwich, Darwin, Dante, Whistler all appear, with others; the historical and ecological poems are well researched and all are gifted with a musical, numinous quality, so that, like the house martin, in the poem of that name, they 'bear the sky home'. Pain is hinted at behind it all on rare occasions, for example 'the years' stored pain crumbles' as it is overcome by the apple-tree in blossom 'that makes a bride of me'. Her mother who died of pancreatic cancer is honoured in a very long, moving, bleakly realistic elegy, 'Poppy in a Storm-struck Field'; and the dangers of radiation affecting even countless children, with no warnings, come across urgently in 'Bird in a Faraday Cage': 'no one's/ counting cancers,// line-breaks in our DNA, our body's/ one small poem'. Wycherley is perhaps strongest in poems anchored in a specific person or situation, often family poems summoning a bygone era. Her poem, Skyline with Chimneys' is dedicated to '*Thomas, brick-burner'*, who is 'the grandfather I never knew/ fed half his life to their flames,/ whistled at dusk as he cycled home'. In 'My Mother arrives in the Fens', the mother is an outsider:

It was not her world:
these catspaws on flooded claypits,
brick-kilns with flickering eyes
weeping brown smoke,

the fen sullen, not yet her friend.

155

Yet, her husband, with 'the fen in his bones,/ the Wash in his blood'

> ...courted her in Brylcream,
> Black-and-Tan. Held her hand
> as she walked on this
> water-made-land. Still queasy.

Many of these poems deserve to be anthologised for ever, such as 'For the Shetland Lace-Knitters' (that appeared in *Agenda*), 'The Apple Tree Woolthorpe'. In the latter poem, the persona is the tree complaining about a rough-and-tumble boy who kicks its apples and climbs its boughs and did at least one day 'say/ my fruit had freed a universe'. But 'no one/ sought the rote of my world'... 'the zenith/ burned through my branches,/ god-gaps where the white stars grow'. Indeed Wycherley unwittingly articulates the undying freshness of her work when, in 'Girl on a Shore', she concludes:

> I'm a young girl again
> impatient for words, like love.

John F Deane

Innocence

I am child of the island, son of its earth, spirit
of Atlantic waters, somepart wolf-soul, somepart

lamb, heather-breezes motherful on my skin, the ever-
sifting-settling sand-clay of its shore like the fretting

in my blood; island, contained, all ocean, mountain, cloud, I
ranging and loping to the overarching obedience

of planet and star, of darkness reaching over sea
to unknown places; soft-silted senses, edged by a landfall

density, my appetites easily assuaged, in the good air and rains,
the fern-world and morass of near-liquid and cold-blooded lives.

I was innocent then, of God, of wickedness or grace, flew
with peewit, lurked with snipe, found the sacred names of things,

the embrace of light and darkness, the fatherful. Till
in preparation for the sacraments they told me sin, told

of the blood, the broken flesh of Jesus, of words mis-matched
to mask the truth, and I found it churlish of the Elders to drag

me in from the sun to a stained-wood pew and cramped
confessional, to tell the wildering trolls of my imagining;

scour, they said, the earthen things, become a dandelion seed
awaiting the Spirit's breath, be stable, stolid, be mainland.

Goldcrest

Of course they come back, the dead, because they are there,
just beyond our being, on the other side
of that nothingness we are scared of, because there is work to do,
on earth and in the heavens,

and because we haunt them. We hear the intricate
tock-tick-tock of the wound-tight
innards of creation: Laudate Dominum, Hagia Sophia, epistolary
symphonies of St Paul.

But our New God is not the Most High God :
he is Burning-bush and Whinny-hill and Furze-bloom; he is not
a gilt tabernacle bathed
in ethereal light – but goldcrest, flitting in the berberis

for a feast of insect while snow
flurries down through a wash of sunlight this out-of-season
Easter week. God
is not *not*: unchanging, unbegotten, ineffable, God is *is*. So I

– remembering days when the pink rose
rambled, and blackberries plashed purple kisses on my lips – find
contentment this side of nothingness, and being
ghosted by the presence of those I have loved, and lost.

Moya Cannon

Mountain Streambed

The bog is cracked and red-gold
and, where the stream has laid bare
half its stone bed.
The quartzite is fluid,
persuaded by the nuances,
the stutterings and inflections,
of the element with which
it has communed for millennia.

Here, a white streak of quartz interrupts
long, tender slopes of stone,
scoured and scored by rounded rocks
now nested in dry pools –
a descending stream of quernstones,
which grind nothing
but time.

I lie down in a stone bowl
in the sun-warmed streambed,
my head beside the flow,
and let the blethering
of mountain water
erode.

Kilcolman

Great force must be the instrument but famine must be the means, for till Ireland be famished it cannot be subdued ... (A Brief note on Ireland)

In my palm lie three rabbit bones
picked white by an owl who carried them home
to this last tower of a castle where a poet
praised his queen in limber verse.
Here, banks now brim with primroses
in a spring which is late and most intense;

here cattle fields are electric-fenced,
mallard and moor-hen nest on the lake
and steps descend to a covered well;
here, Spenser knew little peace,
gave little in return, but laboured to praise
the power which brought him into this place.

From here his grandson would send to Lord Cromwell,
a plea against banishment to Connaght,
would write that, having come to the age of discretion,
he had renounced his mother's popish religion,
and, in that western province, would be placed in peril
as his grandfather's writings 'touching
on the reduction of the Irish to civilitie',
had brought upon him 'the odium of that nation'.

How barbarous the price of courtly ways,
the castle torched, a new-born child dead,
the poet dying in London 'for want of bread';
earlier, the slaughter at Smerwick
and, in subdued Munster, the Irish, starved and sick,
'Creeping from their wooded cover on their hands,
for their legs would not carry them'.
How hard, even still, to love the well-turned verse,
whose felicities were turned on such a lathe.

Sharon Black

Silkworm

You bring me leaves of white mulberry
that I devour, switching
through the bright green pulp, my body growing
Botticelli-plump. Four times I moult, swapping hairs
for talc-smooth skin, each instar
more translucent than the last. You tell me
I am beautiful, run your fingers
over every crease and bulge, cup each tiny
sucker foot, kiss my dun-coloured head.

When I crawl into the cocoon
of our mosquito-netted bed
your hands transform me one last time:
creamy body clasped in a velvet bodice
seamed with gold, dancer's feet,
antennae like enormous lashes quivering
for your attention.

My wings are rice-paper fans
too small to bear my weight.
I have no mouth, will die within five days
but my only need is you, my belly oozing pheromones
we splash upon the sheets.
Instead of a kiss I leave you
this casket of eggs like pinpoint opal beads,
these satin shoes,
this burlesque nuptial gown.

June English

Summer Fruits

I'm sliding sidelong through summer byways
re-igniting moments, sipping the hours;
checking the briars for ripe blackberries –
those first sweet kisses from sun-ripened lips:
the juice, that marked my hands and stained my skirt,
flavoured the wine I brewed in later years:

We're god and goddess, lording over time,
age shall not weary us, nor the weight of years.

I'll nurse the asp to life, teach it new tricks –
the art of love is tenderness and truth –
too many spills between the cup and life,
the discontented snake that fled my bed
slithered illicit byways, snapped elastic –

you filled more nests than mine with fertile seed,
but how the crop that ripened in my womb
adds sweetness to the regret of passion's couch;
at sixteen black was black: those cheating hours,
when you declared your love through lying teeth,
led me to think I'd hate you all my life –

I've learned to harvest sunshine, preserve soft fruits,
your son has eyes like yours, but steady hands,
he helped me brew the wine of sun-ripe berries;
taught me a motherhood of loving.

Deborah Moffatt

The Christian Door

A Christian door, your mother called it,
and you bowed your head before the cross
formed by the muntins and rails
of a door kept closed more often than not.
There was something sacred, you imagined,
in the secrets of that forbidden room –
the stifled whispers, the shuffle of sheets,
the creak of a bed-spring in the night –
and something of heaven and hell
in the storms that blew open the doors
with bright peals of laughter
or the shrill fury of angry words.

The barn, dark and cold and silent,
was a more pagan place, where dumb beasts,
amid blood and manure, silage and hay,
were born and died. The barn door,
heavy and hard to pull on its rusted rails,
was never closed, until that summer day
when you found it nearly so, and slid inside,
to find your father dangling from a beam
with swallows buzzing round his head.

In the swallows' taunting chatter
you heard your mother's mocking laughter;
in the dark silence of the barn
you heard the whispered secrets of the bedroom.
The cross on the door was a coincidence,
a chance arrangement of pieces of wood,
nothing more, Christian only a word,
the sacred and the profane all the same.

Letters from a lover who doesn't exist

You do exist; we met, in a dark crowded room, a sweat of moisture
glistening nervously on cold damp walls, a thick mist of insincerity
masking dagger eyes and grovelling tongues, impossible,
there, then, to know what was real and what was not.

Nothing was said, that night, about the wife I knew you had,
or about the much younger woman at your side, and I knew,
in an instant, what sort of man you were, and kept my distance,
the threat of inconstancy chilling the air between us.

Letters arrive; you exist, but in another dimension, not mine.
I can't believe in you, any more than I can ever be certain
of whatever happens while I sleep, any more than I can measure
the depth of a shadow or the passing of time.

Like an injured bird left to recover alone in the dark,
your letters are lying in a box on a shelf, and I imagine,
at times, that I hear a rustling in the box, the scratching of a pen,
shadows rising from the dead, time, running out.

One day I will open the box and find that the letters have vanished,
that there is nothing left but a few strands of withered words,
an untidy nest of dried ink, a hard little nugget of spent affection
as indeterminate and unqualifiable as a cuckoo's egg.

David Kerridge

A Hospital Wall in Paris

After scullion Gaspard
sluiced *Javel* across the tiles
chemically laving
the barflies' feet, they set to keening
disconsolate in frit
and fretful swill.

By then conjubilant, gabbing
pentecostal in the noonday heat
we girded straight from bar
to street; behind the hospital wall
we heard the chant of shafted riders
crossing the Ebro or charging tanks ...
which was when I said

'Good wall for shooting people against.'

Five metres high of soot-poxed
sandstone, striated by poisoned rain,
it's banged up the sick,
the mad and those who knew not
what their fingers had printed,
who had nobody with, no kin
to take them in ...
and you replied

'Knew you'd say that.'

Recollection

(in memory of François Sommaripas)

Soon, it was proclaimed
the king
would return to his counting house,
the queen
eat bread and honey
and the maid
be back in her rightful place.
In the meantime ...

Flaunted bed-sheets
sopped red
in the dog-bites of wind.
The soldiers gave not a fuck.

'Scobie' you spit the sibilant,
calling up that winter
of '44, and bullets
smacking around the square.
Bidden again to muster,
no more amok nor clawing
at the ground, glittering
shades of the survivors
gather round
beckon you to dance.

Jennie Owen

The Warehouse

Over the years, locks have been added. Rusty bolts that scrape,
alongside shiny padlocks singing with fairy keys. The door is heavy,
chipped green paint, swinging an arc, wide into the dust and dark.

A flick of a switch drowns everything in halogen blaze, floor to roof
boxes stacked in different sizes. Large and scuffed, booming, to
small, wrapped in tissues and silks, thin ribbons in faded colours.

Black rimmed manila envelopes lie in vanilla piles. A dusty tin rattles.
In a baroque gilded caged, labelled 'Past Loves', song birds lie exhausted,
they have long since plucked each other raw, eyes scabbed shut.

I wonder how the origami boxes can be so light, feeling none of the weight
of the ink poured upon them. Others, put to one side an age ago, are huge
monoliths cathedralling. Looming and unmemorable they remain silent.

In the corners, the black spindle legged 'Doubts' catch tiny buzzing 'Ifs'
in coarse webs. Before black dot scuttling away into the shadow
of every casket. Each package beloved or mourned, every one wax sealed.

One day, sledgehammer in hand, crowbar glinting violence, I will return,
split wood, rip squealing hinges, confront my contents. But for now
I quietly polish the wood, whispering and cooing to miscarried endings.

To skin a rabbit

With two pale arms held at noon
or witching hour, together you
and I, skin this bunny rabbit.
Then rough hands, stained
purple with blackberry juice,
chaff the cold prickled skin.

After you go, I watch a while
at the dark, trees suddenly bare;
listen to the breeze, thin and thready,
wishing that fur only grew within.

Time travelling

Slip-sliding, the moment sucks, tugs at you,
lingers wetly on the mouth. You're nearly there,
rubbing your face in the warm fur of its belly,
running fingers over corrugated teeth.
The past
a mirrorball; its chinks of flashback
spiking the nerves, prickling peripheral recall.
You ghost, you coast, and you've arrived.
Not back. Not really.
But nearly.
Shaky legged.
A spinning, quivering, siphon;
travelling too far,
too fast.

Clare Best

Rock fence, County Clare

We know split-rail, ha-ha, painted picket,
spear-top, chainlink, moat, stockade,
double razor, barbed wire, concrete,
snow fence, living fence (cut and laid).
This rock fence where we sit and stare
through thin air at the Burren's edge
is stacked with lichen, mist and shade –
more gap than rock, in fact, the fence
keeps nothing in and nothing out
but hanging there, begins and ends.

Stanton Prior to Lewes

Tonight her car's an apple barn –
she steers the hoard of Bramleys
two hundred miles through wind and rain.

Back home, she lays them out like autumn days,
each green world patched with gold and brown.

The scent returns her to another place –
white-sugared air, black windows streaming
apple syrup, her mother at the stove.

Antony Mair

The Lift

With my ear against the wood, I'm walking slowly,
left arm on Paul's shoulder on the other side,
in step with Johnny at the front – not fast enough for you,
who loved riding against the wind's buffets,
Marie behind you, arms around your waist:
moments of laughing youth, caught and pinned
in the album shown me at the wake, while you
lay framed in satin, with the rosary
threaded round your waxy hands;
                                    we trudge
between the spotless cars and tidy lawns,
swaying rhythmically from side to side,
                                  like the pendulum
to which our sad lives dance; behind us, in disorder,
a loose tangle of the bereaved,
with looks of shattered glass.

Then through the wood I hear your voice, inches away,
Belfast vowels freed from the tumour's rasp:
It's all irrelevant. Don't be afraid.
And suddenly it's as if we're carrying you
        on a slow motion lap of honour, silent-screened,
        and you not raising fists in triumph
        but quietly smiling to discover
        that everything
                – the sitting-room's swagged drapes,
                the power-hosed terraces, the conifer's dwarf arrogance,
                the shining splendour of the Goldwing trike
                abandoned in a nearby garage,
                even the priest's tight-woven certainty –
is wasted effort, mere distraction from
the harder but essential task
                          of love,
an energy that casts out fear and carries you
without our labour, in some other place.

And yet:
        what's continuity for you
is severance for us. Your life's excised from ours,
and as your weight's transferred to other shoulders
for another lift, we're left behind,
        caught in swirls of darkness, standing on the edge
of a precipice we'd turned our backs to,
        but from which we're falling now,
                mouths opening to howl with pain.

William Bedford

Tonight, in these Winter Woods

for Trisha
(October 1962)

Tonight, in these winter woods,
our secret hiding places shake
to an east wind, coldly and bleakly
anchored as the storm breaks.

All night, watching shadows
on the window-panes,
I shiver at a dozen furies:
the footprints of women on the lawn,

the transport planes preparing
for their flight. At my side,
your quiet breathing calms the dark.
Your sleep contains the tide.

Then morning, as it trespasses
our landscapes, glistens with a bright,
unshaken dew, like nightmares,
soon forgotten as the night.

Clive Donovan

Soft Centre

Somehow, the men soften outlines
And insinuate the lenient centre
Whilst the women, brittle at the edges,
Play a little more outside among the
Fringes of the fold where the frigid winds
Moan ancient wails of warning:
Beware! Take care your secrets, women,
Even while you wash your hair and clothes the red
Rocks are listening
For in the untwisting of your braids
Are histories and tales you may not want told.
This wind blows wild seeds that lodge and grow
Neglected in the hems and pockets of your skirts.
Heed this: Your children will repeat the songs and skirls
Of all the chanted laments you consign
To the lacquer boxes of your hearts.
The mysteries are many-knotted
In the padlocked puzzle-cupboards of your minds.
Come back in, come back to that soft centre chamber
Wherein the waiting men expect the clouts
And un-tender thumping lash
For all their traditional crimes.

D V Cooke

Etruscan

At night in the extreme
Early flowering end of April,
I dreamt you alive, that you came back
As a swallow to haunt this locale, dipping
And swerving through the classic dark.

Nothing's as cold as April light
Where everything should be safely
Flowering. The mapped land is not
So quiet. The conduits are dry.
The distant sound of a train pleases
Oddly and rouses life to ember.
That late summer we journeyed south
And blackberrying you goosed our
Hands and faces dark with juice of
The flowering currant and made us
Play at being other than we were
By birth – of entering into that
Darkness. Yet the Christmas after there
Was no star for our nativity.
All had been sold or servile to
The market set. Those hopes we had, not
Dashed, no, but set aside. Thankfully,
In time we learnt to fail, to thresh
And gather those higher meanings,
To find that no self in time will do.

Here, only a small life-like flame
On the gas-stove burns. There's
Nothing of the rococo here. It's all
Exquisite. There's a small pre-Christian
Second century lamp. Nothing too
Twenty-first century. All Etruscan – and
The walls are pastel coloured with the dancing
Dead on their great death journey.

Yet at evening when the swallows again
Surface, we still hear your computer print
Its staccato rhythm, semaphoring
As if from some distant place
We cannot know nor name.

Somersby

Is it for this the choirs sang
And gardens burnished their flower,
Taking the cause of sea or air
To burn and braid the mind a prayer?

And mind is a pulsing presence,
And dust is risen by its tread,
And wheels roll the slow sad earth
And feet are pressed down on the dead.

And the white-faced waves go by,
And pale-ribbed bathers are let be,
And the sun is a gleaming coal
That dies and is quenched in the sea.

A garden is found in the mind
Where death has buried its dust,
Where heart and blushing face may find
Flowers that grow from the waste.

And there when the small ships return
From their journey over the sea –
Talk is only of those who mourn
And the voyages yet to be.

The Sleepers

Dear heart in the night-time finding
As no other love betrays, sing
First of human unsuccess
And then persuade us we may bless.

Who weeps from the tallest window
And watches the darkened river?
The sleepers sleep. They can do
Nothing. Their lives are other.

Who will remember us, they cry –
Our bones rest here and then we die?
Brambles have covered the plot
And greened over what man forgot.

When the shrouds wept down their leaves
And pavement glistened and grievers
Grieved, who paced the unleavened street
Where voices sang some low deceit?

Dear through the night-time shining,
As boats are surging out from shore,
Who will journey for a ring –
Who will answer *neither nor*?

Tony Roberts

Orphée et Eurydice (1859)

Ivan Turgenev to Pauline Viardot, preparing for her role as Orphée.

I miss Spasskoye's old, dark-gold alleys of lime
And the sudden cloudburst of nightingales,
Water dripping from the muzzle of a cow
Beside a pond, sunlight lagging on a lane,
Birch buds, summer straw, wild strawberries.
My ache though is for you –at Courtavenel,
At Baden Baden, charades and cadenzas,
The scents and spirits of each vivid house.
We look back to place when we look to love –
Recitative burnished to aria.
A day not opened by your eyes is lost.
If you will not take me,
       Reçois donc mes derniers adieux,
       Et souviens-toi d' Eurydice...

Simon Jenner

Handel in the Arcadian Academy

Last year, lusts were proper, my lines all wild.
This academy tries me in Theocritus.
All's balanced with Virgil –
pastoral hesitates across an echo:
equal male and castrati. Damned Pope,
banishing last season's women to be scaled

by Venice or Naples. Rome's cardinal lust
is a state for old men. I'm twenty three,
but to their brown eyes a boy. Above
me are none.

Ottobone, Pamphili, the shepherd
princes pursue me; I notate
their gold-dropped pleasures in *Hendel,*
non puo mia misa.
It's the castrati
nymphs
I give to Pasquinini.

So Pamphili can adore me through Ovid –
His Orpheus forswears women for peachy boys,
volumined in his rose silk pounce.
Panalphili trialled it in *Trionfo*
e del Distuango – me as *Un leggiadro*
giovinetto, he flutes off in Neapolitan sixths.

He's even Polyphemus lusting for Acis –
I'll set him again back with Galatea
in another country. Rumpy Rumpoli
made his women wail, abandoned to dissonance.
I crushed chromatic grapes to their white skins,
Ariadne to Hero plunged to taste salt.
Rumpoli twitted me as Amintas, had me breathe
my own Phyllis to him. But he lists
for Phyllis in soprano flesh. Trusts
I share his shiver of a joke.

If I stay, I'll turn Scarlatti. His son
Domenico will, almost my twin.
They'd like me to set
Castor e Pollux, Ganymede,
my flesh eternal marble to the city. *Beloved*
Saxon, blond with your broad sword shoulders,
ravish our senses with yours.

Always an echo chamber, or a night's
blazed pavilion drawn down with draped satin.
Pull it away, then, reveal the naked singing,
young fates I've erected for your stomachers.
Ask nothing of where in the north my tastes lie.

Erratum: Half of this poem only was printed by mistake
in the Poetry & Opera issue of *Agenda*

Tim Murdoch

Full Moon Rising

You are at home among your admirers,
who listen, rictus faced: stone gargoyles
carved on the lintel of a medieval church
rapt with attention, mouths contorting
in the unearthly stages of ecstasy
as musculature strains to keep a hold
on the joyful excesses of liberation.

To those you confide – confident of
their awkward animal love … and yet,
as her soft light slides through the house,
rooms fall silent, suspicion is aroused …
Her refusal to admire us is palpable,
as if she wants yet more; inexplicable
and almost dangerous. Friendship perhaps.

The Cult

She fights his battles for him in his sleep,
he guides her hopes by radar through the gloom,
old needs are previous – deities to keep,
he takes possession of her empty room.

His genius is such that he excels
at every task he gives attention to;
although he knows without her potent spells
he'd come to nothing – and she knows it too.

Graham Hardie

Rosie

Rosie the hills are yours,
the mountains hear your name,
the sea urchin calls you,
and I the poet of all vanity
seek the solace of your realm.
Rosie the waves cover your face,
And the sun shows your light,
When man is manifest in darkness.
To know you is to love you –
the motto of life and you bring life
to those who have none.
Rosie the sky is your mistress,
the sea your God,
and the wind your messenger,
proclaiming that all that is love
shall be love, from air to earth
and from fire to water – as the world
commands your words and deeds.

Gerard Smyth

The Memory Stick

All that was expected did not happen.
What we were most certain of never occurred.
It's all there on the memory stick:
where we were and what we did.
One day we were school leavers,
out the gate and gone in a hurry.
Those were days we wore dark colours
but still believed in the Light of the World
at the end of a summer when we carried
those books we borrowed but never returned
and shut out the world's disturbing news
by listening to Radio Luxembourg.

We let April pass, it had served its purpose –
grabbed with both hands summer's clover.
When our wedding meal was over
we rushed away from the long high table
to the honeymoon shore of pebbles and sand.
We composed our anthems on floors of raw wood
and soon after that discovered a short-cut
home to our cul-de-sac,
the house where we lay our heads
and spoke the praises of two March children,
breastfed at first, then weaned on words
and storybook tales out of this world.

Golden Wonders

They were watching the hayfields becoming abundant.
For the boiling pot they uprooted the crop of *Golden Wonders*.
They spoke in the language of where they were born –
an open house on the road to Cavan and Monaghan.
They had lived through commotions and troubles,
frugal winters, cold comforts. This was the old country
in the old days – nights of looking into the fire,
listening to the rafters creak; the roads were desolate,
strangers seldom seen, maybe a cyclist pedalling hard,
face flushed, remembering stories about the ghosts of Pikemen
on their way to Kilmainhamwood.
At night the first to sing was the one who staggered in,
an ardent singer, back-of-the-chapel Sunday worshipper
down on one knee for the final blessing but gone in a second
                                        before the *Ave Maria*.

Wei Yingwu

(737-792?)

West stream, Chuzhou

only I love the plants that grow
concealed beside that mountain-stream

where deep within the overhanging green
a yellow oriole sings –

spring tides, swollen with rainwater,
pulse swiftly past at dusk:

an empty ferry, not a soul in sight ...
it crosses on its own

Translated by **Kevin Maynard**

Bertolt Brecht

Tahiti

The schnapps ran into the toilet
Down the pink venetian blind.
Tobacco, the life of enjoyment!
Tahiti, three sheets to the wind!

We sailed on a mattress of horsehair:
Stormy night, mountainous sea.
We lurched and the night shipped water,
We were seasick, six of us three.

Fags and schnapps, flush-pump and paper,
Canvas bedding for Topp to mind...
Strip off, Gedde! Hot, this Equator!
Grab your hat, Bidi! Gulf-stream wind!

Cape Good Horn, the waters were stinking,
Java pirates! The ice-green moon.
Skyline, three cannibals singing
'Nearer my God!' The typhoon!

Past Java the schnapps got flowing:
Bidi shot Topp, drumhead-legal.
Gedde's brat, by a passing seagull!
Tradewinds, north! – but the trio kept going.

Translated by **Timothy Adès**

The Drowned Girl

When she was drowned she floated on and on
Down the streams and brooks and into the great big river
The opal light of heaven most splendidly shone
As if impelled to do the body a favour.

Grappled and held by the water-weeds and the slimes,
Slowly and out of proportion her weight increased.
Fishes swam coolly along beside her limbs.
Last haul! as a ferry for green-stuff and water-beast.

In the evenings the sky was as dark as smoke
With the stars by night it kept the light in play
But the brightness came on early when morning broke
So she still had the start and the finish of the day.

As her pallid corpse lay foul in the water there
By God himself she was little by little forgotten:
First her face, then her hands, then finally her hair.
She was just more meat in the water, decayed and rotten.

Translated by **Timothy Adès**

Richard Ormrod

Truffling

'Much have I travelled in the realms of gold'.
Keats

Rooting, snuffling and grubbing
in the cryptic mud of my mind
trying to find a truffle-gem, a poem,
I dig, mole-like, blind –

Sniffing, sifting, clawing the soil
on the alert for the slightest
whiff, nose deep-pressed
in the dark dank earth, lest

despite delving, gouging and probing
the elusive wealth, black-gold
like oil, should foil, escape me –
or grasping, I lose my hold

on its squelchy surface, earth-clogged
like iron-ore before cleaning –
but this find, when refined, is
the gourmet-gold of meaning.

Dens

A poem is a place
I shelter in: dark, secret,
warm – almost like a womb;
or, child again, a hide or den:
a canopy of coats between chairs
a rude tent to camp in
(playing at explorers or Dan Dare);
or high in the sky of the tree-
house, lost among leaves;
re-emerging hours later, as though
I'd never been away: *they*
barely noticing my absence...

or later, an allotment shed
during a downpour: crouching
among the tools, pots, packets
of compost for veg waiting to be fed,
seeds desperate to be dug in;

later still, a book-lined study
in a staid house, cocooned
from neighbours' noise, dogs
or phones: cloistered as any monk
or hermit, waiting for the holy
grail of words: the only lasting den
I still seek refuge in.

Omar Sabbagh, now a well-established poet and critic, was a former young *Agenda* Broadsheet poet.

Poetic Logics

Sinéad Morrissey: *Parallax (Carcanet, 2013)*
Michael Symmons Roberts: *Drysalter (Jonathan Cape, 2013)*

The discussion which follows of Sinéad Morrissey's latest (T.S. Eliot-prize-winning) Carcanet collection, *Parallax* has three major parts. First, a fleshing out of the eponymous theme; second, a highlighting of those moments in the collection where the poet shines with virtuoso colour, whether while instantiating the eponymous theme or not; and third, some (far more minor) criticisms, which latter may be taken to be valid only because the stakes are set so high.

In the Oxford English Dictionary definition given as the epigraph to the collection, we learn that the concept of 'parallax' is in essence the idea that the apparent nature and position of any intended object is displaced by the change in the position of observation. In one sense, to be fleshed below, the idea – hailing from Nietzsche or a scenic Henry James, a 'lying' Oscar Wilde – is that at every point in space, the story (time/narrative) changes. And ranging point of view or what narratology calls 'focalization', is at the heart of some of Morrissey's won effects. That said, difference, in whatever sense, makes no sense unless there is a commonality, however thin, which allows us to dub and render difference.

So, for instance, the collection's opening poem, '1801' is made up of three staggered/sectioned stanzas, which begin with a 'cloudless morning' vista, move to 'afternoon airy and warm', and ends with 'visited evenings... sharp with love'. The final image in the final line runs: '...the new moon holding the old moon in its arms.' This ending highlights both the passage of time (the three sections) and the unifying recursions of time structured by memory – the final words of all three sections are: 'alms,' 'alarm', 'arms' – time regained, then. In one sense, by suggesting how that final line sums up the whole poem, enacts it, I am suggesting that feature of what we might call 'necessary' poetry which is over-determination, a taut, but still fertile, hanging-together of things.

Analogy, like parallax, works by suggesting difference, but as the ripest fruit of unity. All the sliding points of view, however differential and displacing, are dependent on the 'objectivity' so to speak of there being the very (many) subjective points of view. Whether it's the poet's persona

189

hearing 'In other noises...my children crying' ('Baltimore') or, much later, the intriguing idea that 'Death was so much closer' for her 'younger self', when she'd a more over-determining fantasy regarding her future, as 'dead already' or 'at least a grandmother' – the change or shift in point of view, whether spatial or temporal, is dependent on an overall executive intentionality. Another good example comes at the end of (already-cited) 'Baltimore'. The 'infant sleep' at the end of this poem about children, is both the putting to rest of the other, the infant, and the mother as penning poet putting poem to sleep. Two mothers, one child; two children, one mother...

Another way perspective shines through the collection is as the conceit of the penultimate poem, 'A Lie', has it: namely 'That their days were not like our days, / the different people who live in sepia'. Which is to say the passage of time continuously and radically alters sense; a caught image in a photograph here images the fictiveness of, if not the past, our only point of access to it. And this idea is fleshed out here and there in the collection as both liberating (poetic in its essence), but also as dangerous.

So as an example of the way the decaying of time allows for healthy liberating 'lying' (Wilde's term for Jamesian 'scenic selection'), we have the poet's persona in 'The High Window' writing as 'requested' (from a lover's point of view) 'a Raymond Chandler spin-off, / a spoof in style, but from the blonde's perspective.' This leads to an entertaining and colloquial bit of poetic fun. However, in 'The Doctors', we scent the bad 'pun' simultaneously – in the sense of a Stalinesque doctoring and airbrushing of the past. Such crimes against memory and/or commemoration are just as much the consequence of that textuality rendered unavoidable by the passage of time, as the ability to read new pasts, which mean new presents, which empower us poetically or symbolically to carve (a healing and) a new future.

Another kind of sliding or eliding of perspectives is apparent in the (both) use of ekphrasis and (at the same time at times) the poetic reflection on that very use. So in 'Photographs of Belfast by Alexander Robert Hogg' we learn of how 'One cannot tell / if the room in the photograph / entitled *Number 36* // is inhabited' ... That inability to tell is actually telling (in both senses). But the poet is more emphatically sovereign in 'Shostakovich'. Not only is this a poet (Morrissey) writing of and as Shostakovich – a nominal ekphrasis – but the foil within the poem (Shostakovich) ends with a fantastic couplet: 'In all my praise and plainsong I wrote down / the sound of a man's boots from behind the mountain.' That's flair (for both artists). A bit like the ending of 'Migraine' (another poem which uses outer space as vehicle for inner story and storytelling):

I can no longer see your face.
Posed in unravelling sleeves
and disappearing lace,
I have given up all hope for what was whole –
the monkey under the orange tree,
the tatterdemalion nightingale.

Not only is this vanishing hope rendered hopeful, but those last two images, Simic-like or Stevens-like, are suggestive of how after time renders the 'whole' inaccessible, the poet (very poetically) embraces this point of view and, by so vividly highlighting it, simultaneously suggests the necessity or objectivity of all of us having or being limited to a point of view. Indeed, the entertaining conceit of 'Puzzle', a playful rendering of a pat childhood arithmetic riddle ends, in the sestet of the sonnet, like Samuel Johnson's riposte to Bishop Berkeley, by going off on a tangent, goofing off in a manner of speaking.

As yet I have suggested how the poise and control of the poet renders some fantastic effects, and makes us 'see' in many different and differential ways, spatially and temporally. However, at times, and far more rarely in the collection, the poet's craft seems slightly flawed. An example might be 'Lighthouse'. In this poem, we have the prime instance of the eponymous theme: a lighthouse, we read, 'blinks and bats / the swingball of its beam, then stands to catch, /then hurls it out again beyond its parallax.' Light and house; (the very condition of) seeing (at all) and grounded, de-limited perspective; Logos and epilogue; unity as the condition of multiplicity. Indeed, this just quoted image is far from censorable. However, for all this just-cited brilliance (lighting up the poet's home and hearthside with flair), we have one of a few examples where the micrological detail is better than the whole conception; or puts into relief the overall failure. 'Lighthouse' opens with 'My son's awake at ten, stretched out along / his bunk beneath the ceiling, wired and watchful.' Not only is this opening flat, too deadpan in relation to the attempt at profundity which entails, but it is also a stale representation of teenage-hood. To boot, if we are being critical, it would seem de trop to mention in a poem how his 'bunk' is 'beneath the ceiling'. It would have to be. It is only the overall thoroughgoing success of the collection which makes moments like this glaring. They are rare.

Another instance is the last poem 'Blog': pure bathos when related contrapuntally to the wholly successful opening '1801.' And yes, it is intentionally bathetic, given the theme/title, but it is a let-down all the same. We end with 'My good friend Jack told me to write it down.' It's a weak ending to a weak ending. Far from that 'Fool's Gold' (highlight, in this critic's point of view, of the whole collection) which is redolent with alchemical bonding, loving election, where the penning persona *knows*

> the trick
> to set me there,
> my newfound noble elixir,
> the needle to be passed through,
> the famed alchemical ingot
> I could not do without –
> was you.

This wonderful ending to a wonderful poem had me thinking of another love-lyric, 'The Thieves' by Robert Graves, which – a muddle and not a muddle – in its middle runs:

> After, when they disentwine
> You from me and yours from mine,
> Neither can be certain who
> Was that I whose mine was you....

*

Something strange happens when logic becomes poetic logic: senses are conflated, equivocation and ambiguity become vehicles of sense, clear and distinct distinctions are evaded or elided. As an example, and taking a very basic Freudian perspective: it just so happens that a man who expects (too) much attention, narcissistic supply, who wishes for a kind of omniscience or omnipotence – wishes to be always desired via the (infinite) mirror of the other. Now the 'fact' of the matter is ambiguous: two diametrically opposed scenarios result in said symptom. Either said neurotic has had too much attention: thus expects it as his due; or he's had too little: thus strives after it continuously to compensate for its (sometime) lack. This example evinces a poetic logic. Analytical logic would aver that two (strictly) opposed meanings cannot lead to an identical consequence. However, poetic logic thrives on these conflations; nay, makes use of ambiguity to amplify meaningfulness. And this kind of eminently poetic logic I find exemplified throughout Michael Symmons Roberts's superb collection, *Drysalter*.

In the opening poem (the first of one hunded and fifty fifteen-line poems) 'World Into Fragments', we start with the 'Small breaks.' This is 'a world more fragile than we thought.' This fragility is crystallized however, in such potent images as 'great forests disassemble like mosaics,' and 'sun and moon as vast burst bulbs.' Indeed not only is a discordant world congealed thus, but look closely at the workings of the sensibility. The sibilants in 'forests' and 'disassemble' and 'mosaics'; the vivid assonance and consonance of the second citation – formal flamboyance and control typifying the collection. What these lines signpost is a sensibility that is both necessarily passive, that is, following the matter of language, and also at the same time (the sheer coherence of the images) indicates an authorial control which tallies with it, paradoxically, poetically. Indeed, throughout the collection, Roberts seems to find ways of being both poignant and filled with quiddity (15 lines being one beyond the propriety of a sonnet) and universal (150 divided by 15 is 10). Like Eliot, he finds the ability to philosophize in concrete images, beyond the supposed bad taste of (discursive) 'ideas.'

The next two poems in the collection are immediately continuous in their equivocal juxtaposition. 'Something and Nothing' (a title repeated in the collection, as if to compound the antinomy) opens with a 'dancer in the woods' whose 'breath' quickens 'on the breeze.' She is both something then, but also: windily spent. At the end the poet goes 'to her, since I know no better.' A metaphor then for the poignancy of verse (a dancer in the forest), and the fact that it might not 'matter' ('breath' exhausted, by the 'breeze'). The poet who goes to her goes to her from (poetic) need, as well as because there's no other alternative. Poetry is both a bounteous luxury and a staple. The following (contiguous) poem, 'Setting The Trap' is also a metaphor *in toto*, but contains effectual imagery within its architectonics as well. The 'bait' the poet leaves at night is left 'untaken / is removed, the plate washed, table wiped, / and all the vast and empty sky forsaken.' Ignore the rhyme: there is a far more incisive effect here; the concrete (metaphor of) the trap is rounded off with a discontinuous image, the vast and empty sky. Concrete tale and universal sense are tied together in a force-field which typifies successful poetry: that is, in this critic's view, poetry which tells concrete tales and at the same time tales about the very nature and essence of poetry in general. Here the tale about the trap and the bait is a tale leading to the pessimistic ending, in which no-thing is caught, the sky (equally) empty – whether the sky is empty, though, because it just is empty, or whether the sky is empty in a more substantively-intended sense, as 'forsaken', is a question for the reader to negotiate, thankfully.

In 'Ascension' we have a perfect example of said (double) poetic logic; we open with the following stanza:

Because the sun has a dark heart,
the heart must have a dark sun shut inside,
unable to rise or blaze or set.

Ascension, like the idea of 'transcendence' generally, normally betokens objectivity in a philosophical sense. In that, it means 'going beyond' the subjective(ist) prison; going or intending beyond solipsism: being able to reach out to an 'objective' world. And yet here the image is a chiasmus which is both poignant for that 'other' who is the reader, and at the same time denoting (via the paradoxical paralysis) failure to go beyond, 'unable to rise or blaze or set'. Or later, take 'Signs and Portents.' We end this poem with:

When all is said and done it's just a breeze.
I go on daubing words across my house
to *deliver us from*, then I run out of space.

'Signs' then, the gift of 'deliverance,' (an-other kind of ascension or transcendence) by poetry or from evil, as well as the 'portent' that it's just a 'breeze' and that the poet (and his poetry) doesn't 'matter' – especially as he runs out of space, an image of the perfunctory.

Perhaps one of the most beautiful images of this antinomian and poetic logic comes in 'To Listen', where we read of how 'The night sings / in tongues and a black flower / opens inside of us.' Indeed in the recursion of identical titles, throughout the collection (such as, for instance, 'Something and Nothing,' or, 'The Original Zoo') as well as the nominally paradoxical use of titles such as 'Elegy For The Unknown Elegists' or 'The Darkness Is No Darkness', the essence of Roberts's metaphysical sensibility looms out and glares at us. There are also 'Hymns' and pseudo-psalms and self-named 'Songs' throughout, which add a seventeenth century flavour, as in Donne or Herbert. Not to mention the medieval register of some of the songs and hymns, alluded to in the first place by the eponymous 'Drysalter'. These latter conjoin distanced irony and immediate unction, seamlessly, with the seriousness of all true play. But for all the evident intelligence and ratiocination in the verse, that verse is suffused with and spent by concrete, coursing telling.

One might typify the effects of this superlative collection by contrasting two stanzas. In 'Asleep In The Back' we open with (the poetic logic of):

It's dark, by which I mean it's clear enough
to see this child's head rest against
the window, but not to recognize the face.

From that 'hermeneutic circle', then – the idea that every revelation or representation or disclosure (the window) is at the same time operative in hiding something else from view or comprehension (not to recognize the

194

face) – to the closing of, say, 'To An Immortal I':

> For you alone, I make an offering,
> you who have heard it all before,
> I give you this, my mortal song.

The alternation, then, the chequering of touching, nuanced intimation with the (riskier) boldness of a brilliant poet coming into his own.

As I see it, this collection with many faces and with one, is – like, say, Paterson's *Landing Light,* or Heaney's *District and Circle*, or, most recently Wiman's *Every Riven Thing* – a prime example of poetry that is (absolutely) 'necessary'. Which is to say, in one of Roberts's own phrases, the taut conjunction of 'something and nothing': poetry which we never expected; but once there, poetry we couldn't do without.

Belinda Cooke

Dennis O'Driscoll: *The Outnumbered Poet: Critical and Autobiographical Essays*
(Gallery Books, 2013)

This collection of essays reflects the temperament that triggered the numerous accolades that have appeared in the press in the wake of Dennis O'Driscoll's sudden and untimely death on Christmas Eve 2012 – all pointing to his good nature, humour and generosity to other writers. In every sense, the genuine article, like a close friend, he invites you in to share his reading passions and memories of poets he has come across in an intelligent, down to earth, homely, addictive read. In the spirit of Jane Austen's Mr Bennett ('What then do we live for, but to make sport for our neighbours, and laugh at them in our turn'), he pokes fun at absurdities within the poetry scene with an insider's willingness to be the butt of his own jokes – all told with the art of a born storyteller.

There are hints of such self parody immediately in the book's opening section, 'In Person' where far from, say the French tradition of *flânerie* (aimless, reflective strolling) or Wordsworth's wandering 'lonely as a cloud', as a full-time tax inspector his opportunities for 'poetic' strolling are confined to his own estate: 'a side-on view of a corrugated iron warehouse, clapped out Portakabins, bathyspheric tanks. Cavities crater the site, like the boreholes of a mad mineral prospector' ('Walking Out'), all described with the poet's eye. 'In the Midst of Life' he relocates next to a graveyard, less a setting for the muse than a source of dark humour: 'I was never a great admirer of death. I have always regarded it with a healthy disdain ... I would conquer my death phobias by facing down the enemy ... eyeball the headstones and inoculate myself against all thoughts of mortality for the rest of the cheerful day.' Given his recent death, these comments cause the reader a sharp intake of breath, but expect more of this, for such observations feature strongly, variously humorous, poignant or laced with a seize the day attitude to the poetic life.

'Working Bard' debates job security versus going freelance, with the first of his many lighthearted digs at creative writing courses:

> ... how would I survive if my pay, prospects, pension and tenure were to depend, irrespective of the vagaries of a fickle muse, on my being able not only to prove my poethood through regular publications, but also to act as a kind of creative satnav, plotting my students' routes to expressive fulfilment.

He describes the first time he mixed his day job and the muse when asked to write a poem to mark the opening of the Revenue Museum at Dublin Castle and concludes with a seriously held view that it would be presumptuous to define himself as a poet – that is a decision to be made by others – yet he also amusingly notes that it is one step up from admitting to be a tax collector guaranteed to clear the room at a cocktail party.

The bulk of the collection is in Section two 'Poets and Poetry'. It starts with a few more personal pieces and general discussion before going on to pieces on specific poets. 'Making Amends: Assembling a *New and Selected Poems*' is a batch of delightful, painfully accurate aphorisms: 'poets are less wary of *Selecteds* than *Collecteds*, preferring to mark time with a milestone than to call time with a tombstone', and includes this hilarious description of one poem's fate: 'like a pet dog, cruelly abandoned in the hills, which tracks his way home and is grudgingly readmitted to the household'. 'Blurbonic Plague' is packed full of real examples of side-splittingly, dreadful blurbs mixed in with O'Driscoll's imagery on his disapproval of the whole underhand process: 'blurbs clinging like parasitic ticks to poets' collections', 'overheated hogwash and whitewash', 'pressing public valentines on their subjects … for "the best grandmother in the world," ' not to mention the soundbites used to replace the word 'writing': 'and hats off to the poet who… wrenches it into being, slaps it on the page, applies the flames of her passions'. He finally makes fun of creative writing tutors blurbing their students: 'Two doting blurbists, enlisted like godparents at a baptism'. This essay, in particular, is just dazzling in the density of its humorous examples mixed with a more serious invective against what can be mutual backscratching.

His lecture, 'The Library of Adventure', however, is the jewel in the crown of this collection as he takes us through his own personal reading journey. Once read, it will have you dashing off to re-read your Dickens, Austen, Tolstoy – or even loved childhood favourites. From his childhood speed-reading of two books a day to the transition at puberty to slow reader savouring every word, this is an essay that will provide a sharp shock of recognition to all who have that strong desire to know and read everything:

> I sometimes want to bypass the reading process altogether and … simply *inject* knowledge into my veins so that they might course with whatever wisdom or insight the reading of Proust or Plato, Maria Edgeworth or William Faulkner would confer.

The range of this essay is breathtaking in its passion and research as it races through the views and habits of book readers, such as the endless buying of books in a life that is too short. Given the laughter up to this point, one is struck by how absolute his commitment to reading is – slow reading in particular: 'in poetry, rereading is the whole point ... eventually you live in the poem and it lives in you.' He also takes another pop at the teaching of creative writing, this time in the way it can demean reading: 'A kind of booster rocket to be discarded once the would-be author has been launched into inspirational orbit.' He argues that only when we are 'prepared to be challenged and resisted and appalled, as well as charmed and cheered and inspired by what we read are we engaging deeply with literature, opening ourselves fully to its scope', noting also the race against time in such a reading life: 'as if we are barely granted a sidelong glance at the world when it is time to leave it again.'

His next two pieces are concerned with poetry readings. 'The Outnumbered Poet' is another superb lecture. Drawing again on a mesmerizing and eclectic range of sources combined with his own experience, he evaluates the worth of the poetry reading. He kicks off with a mock-serious 'history of the poetry reading which includes great examples of ancient disdain for the practice from Pliny and Juvenal and more recent ones from Leopardi: 'a coarse barbaric vice' and Flann O'Brien's tale of a man who rips his face off when forced to go to a reading. Clearly, throughout history, everyone has wanted to perform but no one to listen. The American poet, Thomas Lynch, tells us: 'if a poet is outnumbered it is a success. If outnumbered by a dozen or more it is huge success'. O'Driscoll mischievously takes him at his word and digs out a story of an island farmer who, out of courtesy, was forced to listen to a poet reading to him when he wanted to get on with his work. To this he adds negative comments from poets who hate readings such as Wallace Stevens: 'poets like millionaires should be neither seen nor heard.'

He proceeds with the shenanigans that go on at readings involving would-be poets and those at various degrees of fame: disputes over who should read first; tales of 'famous poets' putting up with sleeping on floors and that ultimate feeling when you have finally 'arrived' (and here one feels he writes what he has lived), when you his experience the first expenses-paid night in a hotel: 'when the poet rips the plastic hygiene cover from the tumbler and throws open the mini-bar like the door of a Dodge City saloon.' From here, for the 'famous' poet, the problem shifts as expenses are paid but touring means less time to write: 'should they like Enver Hoxha or Saddam Hussein employ look-alike stand ins?' He concludes by coming full circle noting that, in spite of everything, poetry readings still contribute in myriad ways to the poetry community and that as far as reading aloud is concerned we shouldn't forget that most important audience, our inner voice, as we read our work distracted by no one but ourselves.

'Readings remembered' is another densely packed piece taking us back to the start of his earliest memories of poetry read aloud, to his encounters with numerous high profile poets in the years of his work within poetry. His anecdotes are all great fun, such as the tale of how he got a lift to his first public speaking contest by a priest who had met the queen: 'a grand little shtump of a woman, very aisy to talk to,' or the time he tried to contact the current poet laureate c/o Buckingham Palace' assuming he'd live there. Once he meets many high profile poets it is the tight encapsulation of their characters that shine out. We have the funny tale of a very down to earth radio presenter trying to interview Robert Graves who had already developed dementia. He is particularly astute in capturing the essence of Robert Lowell's charismatic appeal:

> Lowell's authority and vulnerability, acuity and frangibility, his paradoxical air of urbanity and otherworldliness bewitched his Kilkenny audience … a model of delivery and presentation which deepened understanding and enhanced appreciation of the work.

Lowell provided him with the most memorable of all his poetry reading experiences citing his advice on the four *musts* of oral performance: 'humour, shock, narrative and a hypnotic voice.' These memories of the above poets and others provide a nice balance to the downsides of readings discussed in 'The Outnumbered Poet'.

The rest of the middle section covers key reviews, retrospectives and more extended pieces on various poets he admires before wrapping things up with the final section on Seamus Heaney's work. Consistently we see him able to paint pictures of the individuals often *in situ* that are both concise and vivid, well-evidenced by the piece on Gallery Press's editor Peter Fallon. He takes us back to Fallon of the early seventies' Dublin bringing poetry out of obscurity: 'His dashing dress code, an exuberant spillage of ink-black hair lent him an aura that was as dandyish as it was hippyish, as mystical as it was modish.' From here he takes us through Fallon's career as a poetic 'mover and shaker' on to his establishment of Gallery Press in Dublin and relocation to his Meath Farm. He also touches on his relationship with his Meath neighbours. In the process he cites the hilarious poem on men caught after drinking 'afters': 'Sure I thought I left ages since.' ('The Late Country'). O'Driscoll is equally insightful on Thomas Kinsella in a piece which, along with describing Kinsella's 'hobby' of poetry by evening and work as civil servant by day, is also very informative on the way Ireland was gradually moving out of its fifties' stagnation and the role of Kinsella's boss, T K Whitaker, Ireland's most famous civil servant in that transition.

The most substantial piece covering the work and life of Michael Hartnett is over 80 pages with the potential to build to a complete monograph. His regular meetings with Hartnett in Dublin throw light on his idosysncracies, alcoholism, brilliance and failed potential. He cites Hartnett's own comments on the influence of his parents: 'I'm dangerous, cantankerous, cranky, a stirrer up of shite and a poet. When you put them all together, you've a dangerous little bundle.' This piece shows Harnett as a gifted maverick with a particular commitment to writing in Gaelic but whose early flowering – producing a selected poems before he was thirty – was curtailed by chronic alcoholism. He notes; 'His writing is quite simply incomplete; an air of unfinished business, of scaffolding still in place'. This is a study that is presented with both affection and deep insight into the mind and work of the poet and is thus very moving to read.

Space does not allow for detailed examination of all the wonderful essays in this collection but they are all consistently on a par with those discussed. Along with his essays on Seamus Heaney, he writes on a diverse range of poets: Billy Collins, Julia Hartwig, Anna Kamieneska, Czeslaw Milosz, Tadeusz Rózewicz, Yehuda Amichai, Douglas Dunn, Vasko Popa, among others, not to mention further essays on unusual topics such as in 'Plumping for Poetry' connections between fatness and thinness in relation to poets or in 'The Widow's Tale' female poets writing on the deaths of their husbands.

It is greatly to Gallery Books' credit, with the assistance of O'Driscoll's wife Julie O'Callaghan and David Wheatley, that they succeeded in publishing this collection within twelve months of Dennis O'Driscoll's life. The contents provide a wonderful testament to a man who clearly had his poetic priorities in the right place. His wit and wisdom offer a restorative tonic, helping one to see what is important to a reading and writing life – the perfect text to sit on any writer's desk.

Biographies

Timothy Adès a rhyming translator-poet, has had over forty Brecht poems published. His books include Victor Hugo's *How to be a Grandfather*, and from Agenda Editions, Jean Cassou's *The Madness of Amadis*, and (in prospect) Robert Desnos's *Storysongs/Chantefables* with pictures by Cat Zaza: both in bilingual text.

Mike Barlow has won a number of competitions, including the 2006 National Poetry Competition. His pamphlet, *Amicable Numbers*, (2008 Templar) was a Poetry Book Society Pamphlet Choice. His third full collection is *Charmed Lives* (Smith Doorstop, 2012). website:www.mikebarlow.org.uk

William Bedford's selected poems, *Collecting Bottle Tops*, and selected short stories, *None of the Cadillacs Was Pink*, were both published in 2009. An essay on 'Ted Hughes and Translation' will be coming shortly from the *Ted Hughes Society Journal*. A new collection of poems, *The Fen Dancing*, was published in March 2014.

Linda Benninghoff graduated with honors from Johns Hopkins University where she majored in English. She has an MA in English with an emphasis on creative writing from Stony Brook. She published five chapbooks of poetry, as well as *Whose Cries Are Not Music*, with Lummox Press.

Richard Berengarten's poetry, most of it available from Shearsman books, draws on and integrates multiple traditions, including English, American, Greek, Italian, Serbian, Chinese and Japanese. Latest books: *Imagems* and *Manual*. Forthcoming: *Notness*, 100 metaphysical sonnets, 2015; *Changing* (homage to the *I Ching*, 2015; and *Richard Berengarten: A Portrait in Inter-Views*, ed. John Dillon, 2016). Recipient of many literary awards in the UK, Macedonia and Serbia, especially for *The Blue Butterfly*. His work is translated into over 90 languages. Bye-Fellow at Downing College, Cambridge. Fellow of the English Association. Poetry editor of *The Jewish Quarterly*.

Clare Best's work has been published in the UK, Canada and the USA. Her first full collection, *Excisions* (Waterloo 2011), was shortlisted for the Seamus Heaney Centre Prize. Clare is currently working with the painter Mary Anne Aytoun-Ellis on a project supported by the South Downs National Park – exploring mysterious and hidden water sources in the South Country of England. Clare teaches Creative Writing at Brighton University and for the Open University. She lives in Lewes. www.clarebest.co.uk

Ruth Bidgood lives in Mid-Wales. She has published 13 collections of poetry. *Time Being* (Seren) won the Roland Mathias prize 2011 and was a Poetry Book Society Recommendation.

Sharon Black is originally from Glasgow but now lives in the Cévennes mountains of southern France. In her past life she was a journalist and taught English in France and Japan. In her current one she runs a holiday venue and organizes creative writing retreats. Her poetry has been published widely. She won Ilkley Literature Festival Poetry Competition 2013, The Frogmore Prize 2011 and was runner-up in the Troubadour Poetry Prize 2013 and Wigtown Book Festival Poetry Competition 2011. Her collection, *To Know Bedrock*, is published by Pindrop Press. www.sharonblack.co.uk

Mark Blayney won the Somerset Maugham Prize for *Two Kinds of Silence*. Stories and poems in *The London Magazine*, *Poetry Wales*, *The Interpreter's House* and others. He has been longlisted for the National Poetry Competition and his story *The Murder of Dylan Thomas* was a Seren Short Story of the Month. Mark is available for mentoring, workshops, MCing and readings: please see www.markblayney.weebly.com

Bertolt Brecht, 1898-1956, a great poet better known for his plays, wrote over 1500 poems, many with rhyme and metre, many not yet published in English. An exile from 1933 in Scandinavia, he crossed Soviet Russia and the Pacific to reach Hollywood, returning in 1948 to East Berlin.

Martin Burke is an Irish born poet (from Limerick) but has lived for many years in Flanders (the Northern Flemish speaking part of Belgium) from where he has published a number of books with small presses in the UK, USA, Ireland, and Belgium.

David Burns grew up in north-east Scotland and is an archaeologist, based near Oxford. His poetry has been published in *Agenda*, *Anon*, *Poetry News* and the anthology *East of Auden*. He was runner-up in the 2008 Faringdon Poetry Competition.

Louise C Callaghan was born in 1948, and grew up in County Dublin. She currently lives in Dublin. *The Puzzle-Heart* was published by Salmon Poetry in 1999; *Remember the Birds*, Salmon, 2005 and *In The Ninth House*, Salmon, 2010. She edited an anthology, *Forgotten Light: Memory Poems* (A&A Farmar, 2003). Her work has been published regularly in *Poetry Ireland Review*, and also anthologized, most notably, in *The Field Day Anthology, Volumes 1V and V*. (2003). She was awarded an M.Litt in Creative Writing specialising in poetry, in 2007 from St Andrews University, Scotland.

Moya Cannon has published four collections of poetry. Her most recent collection, *Hands*, (Carcanet Press, Manchester) was short-listed for the 2012 Irish Times/Poetry Now award. Her work reflects preoccupations with music, landscape, archaeology and with language itself. Her forthcoming collection, *Keats Lives on the Amtrak* will be published by Carcanet Press in 2015. A winner of the Brendan Behan Award and the Lawrence O'Shaughnessy Award, she has been editor of *Poetry Ireland Review* and was 2011 Heimbold Professor of Irish Studies at Villanova University, P.A.

Suzanne Cleary won the John Ciardi Prize for Poetry for *Beauty Mark*, published by BkMk Press in 2013. Her previous books are *Trick Pear* and *Keeping Time*. Her other awards include a Pushcart Prize. She lives in Peekskill, New York, USA. Her website is <suzanneclearypoet.com>.

Belinda Cooke was born in Reading in 1957. She completed her PhD on Robert Lowell's interest in Osip Mandelstam in 1993. She has published three books to date: *Resting Place* (Flarestack Publishing, 2008); *Paths of the Beggarwoman: Selected Poems of Marina Tsvetaeva*, (Worple Press, 2008) and (with Richard McKane) *Flags* by Boris Poplavsky, (Shearsman Press, 2009). She and Richard are currently working on Boris Pasternak's Later poems and her latest collection *Stem* is forthcoming.

David Cooke won a Gregory Award in 1977 and published his first collection, *Brueghel's Dancers* in 1984. His retrospective collection, *In the Distance*, was published in 2011 by Night Publishing and a collection of more recent pieces, *Work Horses*, was published by Ward Wood Publishing in 2012. His poems, translations and reviews have appeared widely in journals in the UK, Ireland, and beyond including *Agenda*, *Ambit*, *The Bow Wow Shop*, *The Critical Quarterly*, *The Frogmore Papers*, *The Interpreter's House*, *The Irish Press*, *The London Magazine*, *Magma*, *The North*, *Orbis*, *Other Poetry*, *Poetry Ireland Review*, *Poetry London*, *Poetry Salzburg Review*, *The Reader*, *The SHOp* and *Stand*. Two Rivers Press will be publishing his new collection, *A Murmuration*, in 2015.

D V Cooke (David Vincent Cooke) was born in Cheshire and graduated in English from London University. He worked for a number of years for The Poetry Library in London and has published in numerous poetry magazines including: *Acumen, Babel, Envoi, Frogmore Papers, Orbis, Outposts, Poetry Wales, Stand, Swansea Review, Tandem* and *Agenda*.

Hilary Davies has published three collections of poetry from Enitharmon: *The Shanghai Owner of the Bonsai Shop*; *In a Valley of This Restless Mind,* which includes poem sequences about the love affair between the 12th century philosopher, Peter Abelard, and his gifted pupil, Héloïse; and *Imperium,* containing an evocation of the naval conflict of the Napoleonic Wars. Hilary won an Eric Gregory award in 1983, has been a Hawthornden Fellow, Chairman of the Poetry Society, and 1st prizewinner in the Cheltenham Literature Festival poetry competition. She was Head of Languages at St. Paul's Girls' School for 19 years and is currently Royal Literary Fund Fellow at King's College, London. Hilary was married to the poet and editor, Sebastian Barker, who died in January 2014.

John F Deane was born on Achill Island 1943; founded Poetry Ireland and *The Poetry Ireland Review*, 1979; published several collections of poetry and some fiction; Won the *O'Shaughnessy Award for Irish Poetry*, the *Marten Toonder Award* for Literature, *Golden Key award* from Serbia, *Laudomia Bonanni Prize* from L'Aquila, Italy. Shortlisted for both the T.S.Eliot prize and The Irish Times Poetry Now Award, won residencies in Bavaria, Monaco and Paris. He is a member of Aosdána . His recent poetry collections: *Eye of the Hare*, came from Carcanet 2011. *Snow falling on Chestnut Hill: New & Selected Poems* was published by Carcanet in October 2012. His latest fiction is a novel, *Where No Storms Come*, published by Blackstaff in 2010. He is current editor of *Poetry Ireland Review*.

Clive Donovan has been writing poetry full-time for four years and has had several dozen pieces accepted by editors of various U.K. hard-copy poetry magazines. He lives in the creative atmosphere of Totnes town in Devon. He has yet to publish a first collection.

Ian Enters is the Chair of Trustees for the charity Reading Matters. His two novels were published by Weidenfeld and Nicolson. *Outposts* and *Envoi* published his three poetry collections. He has also created an opera, a number of musicals and plays. He taught English and Drama for many years in London, Sussex and Sheffield schools. He was Adviser for English and drama and then Arts Education Adviser for Sheffield. He directed Steel Valley Beacon Arts in South Yorkshire until recently. Now retired, poetry is his passion.

June English has written a chapter in *Writing Your Self: Transforming Personal Material* (2009) by John Killick and Myra Schneider published by Continuum. Her first collection of poetry, *Counting the Spots* (2000) published by Acumen was short-listed for the BBC 'New Voices' programme. *The Sorcerer's Arc* (2004) her first full collection was published by Hearing Eye, London, *Sunflower Equations* (2008) was published by Hearing Eye. A new collection is due out later this year. Her poems have been published in the *Daily Mirror* (Carol Ann Duffy's Poetry Corner), *The Morning Star* and *The Guardian*.

Adam Feinstein is the UK biographer of the Chilean Nobel Prize-winning poet, Pablo Neruda. His 2004 book, *Pablo Neruda: A Passion for Life*, re-issued by Bloomsbury in an updated edition in 2013, received widespread acclaim (Harold Pinter called it 'a masterpiece'). His book of translations from Neruda's *Canto general*, with colour illustrations by one of Brazil's leading artists, Ana Maria Pacheco, was published by Pratt Contemporary last year. He is currently working on a collection of translations from the verse of the Spanish poet, Félix Grande, and a book on cultural policy in Cuba since the Revolution. His poems and translations have appeared in publications around the world. In 2013, he launched a biannual magazine, *Cantalao*, dedicated to Neruda's life and work.

Sally Festing's second chapbook is *Salaams* (Happenstance, 2009). She is writing poems about North Norfolk where she runs Saltmarsh Poetry in Burnhams. Her most recent non-fiction is *Showmen: the Voice of Travelling Fair People*.

John A Griffin was born in Tipperary Town, Ireland. He moved to the U.S.A in 1983, where he read for his BA, MFA, MA, and PhD. He now lives and works in Riyadh, Saudi Arabia, where he leads the English Department of his school. John published his first book of poems, *After Love*, in 2012 with Pen & Anvil Press, Boston. He has also published essays and poems in journals, and is currently writing a novel. He has four children.

Graham Hardie's poetry has been published in *Agenda, Shearsman, The Interpreter's House, Gutter, The New Writer, Markings, Nomad, Cutting Teeth, The David Jones Journal, Cake* and online at nth position and Ditch. He is 42, works as a gardener and lives near Glasgow.

James Harpur has published five books of poetry with Anvil Press. His latest collection, *Angels and Harvesters*, was a Poetry Book Society Recommendation and shortlisted for the Irish Times Poetry Prize. He lives in West Cork. www.jamesharpur.com

Mark Harris was born 1962 and currently lives in the North West, beside the coast. Mark spent 18 years working as a communications consultant until last year when his beautiful seven year old son, Miller, passed away. Writing poetry is a way of both managing and reaching beyond personal loss.

Simon Jenner was born in Cuckfield, 1959, making his debut in parallel German/English volumes. Waterloo subsequently published *About Bloody Time* (2006) *Wrong Evenings* (2011), *Two for Joy* (2013); *Pessoa* was brought out by Perdika (2009) who are publishing his close translations of Propertius Elegies Book I. An *Agenda* Edition *Airs to Another Planet* on music poems is also forthcoming. He reviews for e.g. *Agenda, Angel Exhaust, Tears in the Fence* (essays on Oxford 1940s poets, Robert Nye, John Goodby, Mario Petrucci, Jeremy Reed, Geoffrey Hill). He contributed to the *Companion to Richard Berengarten* (Salt, 2011). He has been Director of Survivors' Poetry since 2003, awarded Royal Literary Fund Grants and Fellowships at UEL and Chichester. He has taken up one of the first six Residencies of Poet in the City, in Hackney.

Tess Jolly lives in West Sussex where she has recently become a workshop leader for the Little Green Pig Writing Project. She has had poems published in a wide variety of paper and online magazines including *Magma*, *The North*, *Iota* and *Obsessed with Pipework* and was a runner-up in last year's Mslexia Poetry Competition.

Faye Joy trained as a painter and printmaker at Wolverhampton College of Art, subsequently studied etching with Norman Ackroyd at the Central School of Art in London. For many years she was a teacher of Art and History of Art in East Sussex but now lives in Normandy, France, where she paints and explores various machine embroidery techniques, exhibiting work in a contemporary gallery in Lisieux.Whilst studying with the Open University over the last few years, she has enjoyed two Arvon Foundation Courses in poetry. For several years now, she has written poetry based on childhood reminiscences and walks around Cormeilles where she lives.

David Kerridge was born near London in 1943. He worked at the BMA for six years before moving to Paris in 1970, where he has worked as a teacher, and translator of medical documents. During the 60s and 70s, he had a number of poems and short stories published, and in the last twenty years has written text books for UK and French publishers.

Antony Mair was formerly a commercial lawyer, then a French estate agent. He now lives in Hastings, East Sussex. He has had poems published by *Acumen* and *Ink Sweat and Tears* and is currently engaged in compiling an anthology of poems by members of the Brighton Stanza Group. He is about to undertake a Creative Writing MA with the University of Lancaster.

Kevin Maynard is a teacher of English and Mandarin, currently living in Hertfordshire. He has had poems and translations published in a number of little magazines, and is currently working on a series of historical novels set in Hogarth's London.

Michael McCarthy is a West Cork born poet living in North Yorkshire. A winner of the Patrick Kavanagh Award, his most recent collection *At the Races* was the overall winner of the Poetry Business Competition judged by Michael Longley.

Gill McEvoy runs several poetry events in Chester, including workshops under the name *PoemCatchers*, and Zest! Open Mic poetry nights. Her second collection, *Rise*, was published by Cinnamon Press in May 2013. First collection *The Plucking Shed*, Cinnamon Press, 2010, (now sold out). Website: www.poemcatchers.com

Stuart Medland has written two collections of poems for children, composed whilst still a primary school teacher in Norfolk. Much of his writing is inspired by natural history and his *Rings in the Shingle*, published by Brambleby Books, is a poetic celebration of Norfolk wildlife inspired by his own photographic encounters. *Ouzel on the Honister*, a volume of poems distilled from his many visits to the Lake District over the years, is currently in preparation. Stuart is now a regular contributor to *Agenda* and a collection of poems about his father, *Last Man Standing*, is due from *Agenda Editions*.

Julie Mellor. Julie Mellor's work has appeared in various magazines and anthologies including *Mslexia, The North, Smiths Knoll* and *The Rialto*. Her pamphlet, *Breathing Through Our Bones*, was a winner of the 2011 Poetry Business pamphlet competition judged by Carol Ann Duffy.

W S Milne, poet, dramatist and critic, has just completed translating the whole of Homer's *Iliad* into Scots.

Deborah Moffatt was born in Vermont and lives in Fife. Her poems have been widely published in the UK and Ireland. Her first collection of poetry, *Far From Home*, was published by Lapwing (Belfast) in 2004. She recently won the Baker Prize 2012 and was also included in *Poems of the Decade; an anthology of the Forward books of poetry 2002-2011*.

Abigail Morley's first collection *How to Pour Madness into a Teacup* was shortlisted for the Forward Prize Best First Collection (2010), her second, *Snow Child* is published by Pindrop Press (2011) and her pamphlet *Eva and George: Sketches in Pen and Brush* came out this year. Her work appears in anthologies and journals including *Agenda, Other Poetry, Poetry Review* and *The Spectator.*

Tim Murdoch's poetry has appeared over the years in *Agenda*, and elsewhere. He is preparing a poetry collection for publication.

Grace Nichols was born and educated in Guyana and came to Britain in 1977. She has published many books for both adults and children. Her first poetry collection; *I Is A Long Memoried Woman* won the 1983 Commonwealth Poetry Prize. Her other adult books include: *The Fat Black Woman's Poems; Sunris* winner of the Guyana Poetry Prize and *Startling The Flying Fish* all published by Virago who published her first novel; *Whole Of A Morning Sky.* Her latest collections are: *Picasso, I Want My Face Back* and *I Have Crossed An Ocean'* (both published by Bloodaxe Books). She was poet-in-residence at The Tate Gallery, London 1999 – 2000 and is among the poets on the GCSE syllabus. She is a Fellow of The Royal Society of Literature and her latest collection for young people; '*Cosmic Disco'* was published recently by Frances Lincoln.

Mary Noonan lives in Cork, where she lectures in French literature at University College Cork. Her poems have appeared in numerous magazines, including *The Dark Horse, Poetry Review, Poetry London, Wasafiri, The North, Tears in the Fence* and *The Threepenny Review.* She won the Listowel Poetry Collection Prize in 2010. Her first collection – *The Fado House* (Dedalus, 2012) – was shortlisted for the Seamus Heaney Centre Prize and the Strong/Shine Award.

Jean O'Brien's latest poetry collection, *Merman* (Salmon 2013) was named after her poem that won the 2010 Arvon International Poetry Award. Her work is widely published, anthologised and broadcast is Ireland and elsewhere. She holds an M.Phil in creative writing from Trinity College, Dublin and tutors in creative writing.

Ruth O'Callaghan has been translated into six languages and has read extensively in Asia, Europe and the USA – where she also completed a successful TV/Reading tour in New York and Boston. The Arts Council sponsored her to visit Mongolia to collaborate with women poets on a book and a C.D. and in 2010 to she was awarded a gold medal in Taiwan for her poetry. She is a competition adjudicator, interviewer, reviewer, editor, workshop leader and mentor and is the poet for *Strandlines*, a community, multi-disciplinary project run under the auspices of Kings College, University of London. Her fourth collection *The Silence Unheard* was published in 2013.

Paul Ó Colmáin is a poet, musician, songwriter and visual artist who lives near Ballydehob in West Cork. He is also an Irish language teacher and a tour guide who leads walking tours at home and abroad. He is a regular contributor of poems in both Irish and English to journals and anthologies. He is a member of Cork Printmakers and specialises in wood engraving. He is currently collaborating on a book with poet, James Harpur, illustrating James' poems of Irish Early Christian saints, some of which are included here. www.paulocolmain.com

Jessamine O Connor comes from Dublin, and lives in rural Sligo. In 2013 she was short-listed for the Hennessy Literary Award, the Red Line Book Festival competition, and the Dead Good Poetry competition; in 2012 short-listed for the Bradshaw Books manuscript competition; and in 2011 she won both the *iYeats*, and the Francis Ledwidge awards. One of her poems is installed in the Hawkswell Theatre, Sligo. Publications include *The Stinging Fly, Abridged, The Stony Thursday Book, New Irish Writing,* the *Leaf Books* magazine and anthology *Balancing Act, Ropes, Crannog,* and the online journals *The First Cut, Shot Glass Journal,* and *The Galway Review.* In 2013 she received an artist's bursary to publish her first chapbook *Hellsteeth,* available from www.jessamineoconnor.com

Richard Ormrod is a published biographer, journalist and reviewer. He is currently writing the authorised biography of the poet Andrew Young and is working towards his own first volume of poems. He is married and lives in East Sussex and was, for some years, a Head of English in several schools in Kent.

Jennie Owen is a University Lecturer and has been a Senior Editor for the on-line journal *Black Market Review* since 2008. She has been published in various magazines and is also a member of Skelmersdale Writers' Group.

William Oxley was born in Manchester. His poems have been published in magazines and journals as diverse as *The New York Times, The Observer, The Spectator, The Independent, Agenda, Acumen, The London Magazine* and *Poetry Ireland Review.* A study of his poetry, *The Romantic Imagination,* appeared in 2005 from Poetry Salzburg. His most recent volumes are *ISCA – Exeter Moments* (Ember Press 2013) and *Poems from the* Divan *of Hafez* (translated from the Persian with Parvin Loloi)(Acumen Publications, 2013). His *Collected and New Poems* has just come out from Rockingham Press, 2014. He has given readings throughout the UK, as well as abroad in Nepal, Antibes and elsewhere.

Jeremy Page has edited *The Frogmore Papers* since 1983. He is the author of several collections of poems, most recently *In and Out of the Dark Wood* (HappenStance, 2010). His work has been translated into German and Romanian, and a selection of his poems was recently broadcast on Radio Romania Cultural in English and Romanian. His own translations of Catullus are published by Ashley Press as *The Cost of All Desire.* He teaches at the University of Sussex.

Stuart Pickford teaches in a comprehensive school in Harrogate.

Nigel Prentice has had work published over a number of years in various journals, including *Poetry Review, The London Magazine, The Rialto* and *Long Poem Magazine.*

Robin Renwick was born on a farm in Sussex and studied Design at the Royal College of Art. He has spent most of his working life as a designer/printer and lecturing in Art and Design. He retired from full time lecturing in 2001 and now works as a part-time rock climbing instructor. He has previously had poems published in *Agenda.*

Tony Roberts was educated in England and America. He has published three poetry collections: *Flowers of the Hudson Bay, Sitters* and, most recently, *Outsiders* (Shoestring Press, 2010). His poems, reviews and essays appear regularly in the literary press.

Simon Royall is 36. He grew up in Nottinghamshire, studied at The Norwich School of Art & Design and currently lives in Gloucestershire. His poetry has appeared in *Poetry Review, The Rialto, Ambit* and *Magma.*

Omar Sabbagh is a widely published poet and critic. As well as being a regular contributor to *Agenda,* his poetry and prose has appeared (and often repeatedly) in such venues as: *Poetry Review, PN Review, Poetry Ireland Review, The Reader, The Warwick Review, POEM, Kenyon Review, Poetry Wales, Stand, Wasafiri, The Wolf, Lighthouse, Banipal, The Moth,* and elsewhere. His three extant poetry collections include: *My Only Ever Oedipal Complaint* and *The Square Root of Beirut* (Cinnamon Press, 2010/12). In January 2014 Rodopi published his monograph: *From Sight through to In-Sight: Time, Narrative and Subjectivity in Conrad and Ford.* For the years 2011-13 he was Visiting Assistant Professor at the American University of Beirut (AUB).

Eva Salzman's books include *Double Crossing: New and Selected Poems* (Bloodaxe) and *Bargain with the Watchman* (Oxford) - both Poetry Book Society Recommendations and the acclaimed anthology *Women's Work: Modern Women Poets Writing in English* (Seren) co-edited with Amy Wack. Her essays, features, reviews, fiction and poetry have been published in the *TLS, Spectator, Poetry Review, Independent, Guardian, Times, New Yorker, Kenyon Review* and in numerous anthologies such as the New Writing anthologies published by the British Council in conjunction with Picador/Vintage. Opera libretti include various collaborations and those commissioned by Buxton Opera Festival and English National Opera Studio and an opera written for her composer father which has been performed widely in Europe. She has been writer-in-residence in HMP Springhill, has held fellowships at Villa Mont Noir (France) and Wesleyan Writers' Conference (USA), and been a Royal Literary Fund Fellow at Ruskin College, Oxford and Warwick University. Currently she is Associate Lecturer at Goldsmiths.

Gerard Smyth was born in Dublin where he still lives. His seventh collection, *The Fullness of Time: New and Selected Poems* (Dedalus Press, Dublin) was published in 2010 and appeared in an Italian translation last year. He was the 2012 recipient of the O'Shaughnessy Poetry Award from the University of St Thomas in Minnesota. He is co-editor of *If Ever You Go: A Map of Dublin in Poetry and Song* (Dedalus) which was Dublin's One City One Book this year. He is a member of Aosdána and Poetry Editor of *The Irish Times*.

Will Stone, born 1966, is a poet, essayist and literary translator. His first poetry collection *Glaciation* (Salt, 2007), won the international Glen Dimplex Award for poetry in 2008. A second collection *Drawing in Ash*, was published by Salt in May 2011. His translated works include a recent series of books for Hesperus Press, with translations of works by Maurice Betz, Stefan Zweig and Joseph Roth. His recently published *Emile Verhaeren Poems* will be followed by *Georges Rodenbach Poems* in autumn 2014. Pushkin Press will publish his first English translation of Stefan Zweig's essay on Montaigne in 2015 and Seagull Books an expanded collection of the poetry of Georg Trakl in 2016.

Lynne Wycherley currently lives by a headland and nature reserve in Devon, and has appeared regularly in *Agenda* over the years. Her most recent volume, from Shoestring Press (summer 2104), is *Listening to Light: New & Selected Poems*.

Wei Yingwu (737–c.792) was a poet of noble birth who held office in both Tang dynasty capitals, Chang'an and Luoyang, and who lived through the catastrophic and genocidal An Lushan rebellion: an event which sowed the seeds of the dynasty's decline. He does write movingly about this elsewhere, but is best known for the calm and meditative poetry he wrote either about his natural surroundings or about more personal themes. 'West Stream, Chuzhou' is one such poem.

TEAR–OFF SUBSCRIPTION FORM

Pay by cheque (payable to 'Agenda'), or
Visa / MasterCard

SUBSCRIPTION RATES ON INSIDE FRONT COVER

1 Subscription (1 year) =

2 double issues 1 double, 2 single issues or 4 single issues (The above is variable)

Please print

Name: ....

Address: ....

....

....

.... Postcode ....

Tel: ....

Email: ....

Visa / MasterCard No: ☐☐☐☐☐ – ☐☐☐☐ – ☐☐☐☐ – ☐☐☐☐

Expiry date: ☐☐ – ☐☐

Please tick box:

New Subscription ☐   Renewed Subscription ☐

(or subscribe online – www.agendapoetry.co.uk)

Send to: AGENDA, The Wheelwrights, Fletching Street, Mayfield,
East Sussex, TN20 6TL
Tel: 01435-873703